taste of home

sandwiches
wraps & more!

BURRITOS MADE EASY, PG. 65

taste of home
sandwiches wraps & more!

VICE PRESIDENT, EDITOR-IN-CHIEF:	Catherine Cassidy
VICE PRESIDENT, EXECUTIVE EDITOR/BOOKS:	Heidi Reuter Lloyd
CREATIVE DIRECTOR:	Howard Greenberg
FOOD DIRECTOR:	Diane Werner, RD
SENIOR EDITOR/BOOKS:	Mark Hagen
EDITOR:	Amy Glander
ASSOCIATE CREATIVE DIRECTOR:	Edwin Robles Jr.
ART DIRECTOR:	Jessie Sharon
CONTENT PRODUCTION MANAGER:	Julie Wagner
LAYOUT DESIGNER:	Catherine Fletcher
COPY CHIEF:	Deb Warlaumont Mulvey
COPY EDITOR:	Susan Uphill
RECIPE ASSET SYSTEM MANAGER:	Coleen Martin
RECIPE TESTING AND EDITING:	Taste of Home Test Kitchen
FOOD PHOTOGRAPHY:	Taste of Home Photo Studio
COVER PHOTOGRAPHER:	Rob Hagen
COVER FOOD STYLIST:	Kathryn Conrad
COVER SET STYLIST:	Dee Dee Jacq
ADMINISTRATIVE ASSISTANT:	Barb Czysz
NORTH AMERICAN CHIEF MARKETING OFFICER:	Lisa Karpinski
VICE PRESIDENT/BOOK MARKETING:	Dan Fink
CREATIVE DIRECTOR/CREATIVE MARKETING:	Jim Palmen

The Reader's Digest Association, Inc.

PRESIDENT AND CHIEF EXECUTIVE OFFICER:	Robert E. Guth
EXECUTIVE VICE PRESIDENT, RDA, AND PRESIDENT, NORTH AMERICA:	Dan Lagani

International Standard Book Number (10): 0-89821-977-9
International Standard Book Number (13): 978-0-89821-977-7
Library of Congress Control Number: 2011935877

Printed in China.

Front cover: Turkey Focaccia Club, pg. 43.

Back cover, top to bottom: Ham Pinwheels, pg. 8; Ham and Cheese Calzones, pg. 91;
Cashew Turkey Salad Sandwiches, pg. 54; Whoopie Pies, pg. 106; Aloha Burgers, pg. 28.

For other Taste of Home books and products, visit ShopTasteofHome.com

INDULGE...
IN 192 SANDWICH CREATIONS!

Craving something big and tasty that's a cinch to assemble? A satisfying sandwich stacked high with fresh and flavorful ingredients is sure to hit the spot. Whether you want to sink your teeth into a classic club or slowly savor something hot and tender tucked inside a bun or wrap, you'll find all your favorites plus innovative creations inside *Taste of Home Sandwiches, Wraps & More!*

Hoagies, subs, wraps, roll-ups, pitas, paninis, open-faced delights, breakfast creations, even twice-as-nice dessert sandwiches...these hand-held wonders can be enjoyed at any meal, served alongside a steamy cup of soup or even reinvented from last night's leftovers. And because these recipes call for everyday ingredients, and in most cases take only minutes to create, they're ideal for a relaxing lunch, a light dinner or a dish to pass at a potluck.

Enjoy an enticing assortment, from timeless standbys such as French Dip Sandwiches (pg. 41) and Waffled Monte Cristos (pg. 39) to new taste sensations like Lime Jalapeno Turkey Wraps (pg. 65) and Hawaiian Ham Salad Pockets (pg. 81). You'll even find stromboli, calzones, quesadillas, crepes and other original variations, all proud to be members of the sandwich family!

Packed with 192 recipes, full-color photos and handy tips, *Sandwiches, Wraps & More!* has all the inspiration for hand-crafting the perfect sandwich!

table of contents

BISTRO BREAKFAST PANINI, PG. 16

GREAT GIFT! *Taste of Home Sandwiches, Wraps & More!* makes a great gift for those who love sandwiches and other deli delights. To order additional copies, specify item number **42116** and send $14.99 (plus $4.99 for shipping/processing for one book, $5.99 for two or more) to:

Shop Taste of Home, Suite 523
P.O. Box 26820
Lehigh Valley, PA 18002-6820

To order by credit card, call toll-free
1-800/880-3012

HAM PINWHEELS, PG. 8

appetizer & snack sandwiches

SMOKED SALMON APPETIZER CREPES, PG. 9

CRAB SALAD TEA SANDWICHES, PG. 10

mini beef wellingtons

PREP: 2 hours + cooling | **BAKE:** 15 min./batch
YIELD: 40 appetizers.

*I discovered this delicious party starter at a wedding.
I sampled one and decided to duplicate the recipe at home.
My version is a bit easier and faster to prepare, but just as
elegant and delicious.*

ANNIE DE LA HOZ, DELTA, COLORADO

- 1 boneless beef chuck roast (3 to 4 pounds)
- 14 tablespoons butter, *divided*
- 1 can (10-1/2 ounces) condensed beef broth, undiluted, *divided*
- 1 cup Madeira *or* marsala wine, *divided*
- 1/2 pound medium fresh mushrooms, finely chopped
- 1 garlic cloves, minced
- 3 tablespoons minced fresh parsley
- 2 tablespoons cornstarch
- 1/2 teaspoon salt
- 1/4 teaspoon pepper
- 5 tubes (16.3 ounces *each*) large refrigerated flaky biscuits

1 In a Dutch oven, brown roast on all sides in 4 tablespoons butter. Pour 1/2 cup broth and 1/2 cup wine over roast. Cover and bake at 325° for 1-1/4 to 1-1/2 hours or until tender. Remove roast and cool slightly; shred meat with two forks.

2 In a small skillet, saute mushrooms in 2 tablespoons butter until tender. Add garlic; cook 1 minute longer. Stir in parsley; set aside.

3 In a large saucepan, bring remaining broth and 1 tablespoon butter to a boil. Combine cornstarch and remaining wine until smooth; gradually stir into the pan. Bring to a boil; cook and stir for 2 minutes or until thickened. Stir in the meat, mushroom mixture, salt and pepper.

4 Press each biscuit into a 4-in. circle. Place 2 tablespoons meat mixture on half of each circle. Bring edges of biscuit over mixture and pinch seam to seal. Place on greased baking sheets. Bake at 400° for 15-20 minutes or until golden brown. Melt remaining butter; brush over appetizers.

stuffed bread appetizers

PREP: 20 min. + chilling | **YIELD:** about 2 dozen.

*You may want to double the recipe for this refreshing
appetizer because folks won't be able stop at just one slice!*

TRACY WESTROM, LANSDALE, PENNSYLVANIA

- 2 packages (one 8 ounces, one 3 ounces) cream cheese, softened
- 1 cup chopped celery
- 1 cup (4 ounces) shredded cheddar cheese
- 1/2 cup chopped sweet red pepper
- 1/2 cup chopped water chestnuts
- 1 teaspoon garlic salt
- 1 loaf (26 inches) French bread, halved lengthwise

Mayonnaise

Dried parsley flakes

- 4 dill pickle spears
- 4 slices deli ham

1 In a large bowl, combine the first six ingredients; set aside.

2 Hollow out top and bottom of bread, leaving a 1/2-in. shell (discard removed bread or save for another use). Spread thin layer of mayonnaise over bread; sprinkle with parsley.

3 Fill each half with cheese mixture. Wrap pickle spears in ham; place lengthwise over cheese mixture on bottom half of loaf. Replace top; press together to seal.

4 Wrap in foil; refrigerate overnight. Just before serving, cut into 1-in. slices.

walnut-cream cheese finger sandwiches

PREP/TOTAL TIME: 30 min. | **YIELD:** 3 dozen.

Guests at an English tea my wife and I hosted thought these little sandwiches were fabulous. Even people who are not fond of cream cheese will love them. CHUCK HINZ, PARMA, OHIO

- 12 ounces cream cheese, softened
- 1/2 cup finely chopped walnuts, toasted
- 2 tablespoons minced fresh parsley
- 1 tablespoon finely chopped green pepper
- 1 tablespoon finely chopped onion
- 1 teaspoon lemon juice
- 1/4 teaspoon ground nutmeg
- Dash salt and pepper
- 24 thin slices white sandwich bread, crusts removed

1 In a small bowl, beat the cream cheese, walnuts, parsley, green pepper, onion, lemon juice, nutmeg, salt and pepper until all the ingredients are blended.

2 Spread about 2 tablespoonfuls of the cream cheese mixture over each of 12 bread slices; top with remaining bread. Cut each sandwich into three 1-in.-wide strips.

puffy lobster turnovers

PREP/TOTAL TIME: 25 min. | **YIELD:** 16 appetizers.

Here, tender bits of lobster are nestled in golden-brown puff pastry for an elegant appetizer. BENNY DIAZ, AZUSA, CALIFORNIA

- 1 cup chopped fresh lobster meat
- 1/4 cup finely chopped onion
- 1 teaspoon minced fresh basil
- 1 teaspoon minced fresh thyme
- 1 teaspoon paprika
- 1 garlic clove, minced
- 1 teaspoon tomato paste
- 1/8 teaspoon salt
- 1/8 teaspoon pepper
- 2 packages (17.3 ounces *each*) frozen puff pastry, thawed
- 1 egg, lightly beaten

1 In a small skillet, combine the first nine ingredients. Cook and stir over medium heat for 4-5 minutes or until lobster is firm and opaque; set aside.

2 Unfold puff pastry. Using a 4-in. round cookie cutter, cut out four circles. Place on a greased baking sheet. Repeat with remaining pastries. Spoon 1 tablespoon lobster mixture in the center of each circle. Brush edges with egg; fold dough over filling. Press edges to seal.

3 Bake at 400° for 8-10 minutes or until puffy and golden brown. Serve warm.

tip Puff pastry is a rich dough made by placing chilled butter between layers of pastry dough. It is then rolled out, folded into thirds and allowed to rest. This process is repeated six to eight times, producing a pastry with many layers. Commercially prepared puff pastry can be used in recipes that call for homemade puff pastry dough, such as croissants.

mini muffuletta

PREP: 25 min. + chilling | **YIELD:** 3 dozen.

Guests love the Mediterranean flavor in these mini sandwich wedges. The recipe is great for a party and can be made a day in advance. GARETH CRANER, MINDEN, NEVADA

1 jar (10 ounces) pimiento-stuffed olives, drained and chopped
2 cans (4-1/4 ounces each) chopped ripe olives
2 tablespoons balsamic vinegar
1 tablespoon red wine vinegar
1 tablespoon olive oil
3 garlic cloves, minced
1 teaspoon dried basil
1 teaspoon dried oregano
6 French rolls, split
1/2 pound thinly sliced hard salami
1/4 pound sliced provolone cheese
1/2 pound thinly sliced cotto salami
1/4 pound sliced part-skim mozzarella cheese

1 In a large bowl, combine the first eight ingredients; set aside. Hollow out tops and bottoms of rolls, leaving 3/4-in. shells (discard removed bread or save for another use).

2 Spread olive mixture over tops and bottoms of rolls. On roll bottoms, layer with hard salami, provolone cheese, cotto salami and mozzarella cheese. Replace tops.

3 Wrap tightly in plastic wrap. Refrigerate overnight. Cut each into six wedges; secure with toothpicks.

ham pinwheels

PREP: 10 min. + chilling | **YIELD:** 1 dozen.

I serve these pretty pinwheels with fresh salsa and jalapenos on the side. Pair them with a cup of soup for a light lunch or serve as party starters at your next get-together. DEANNA PHILLIPS, FERNDALE, WASHINGTON

```
1/4  cup refried beans
  2  flour tortillas (6 inches), room temperature
1/2  cup fresh baby spinach
  4  slices deli ham (3/4 ounce each)
  1  hard-cooked egg, chopped
  2  tablespoons shredded sharp cheddar cheese
  2  tablespoons shredded Monterey Jack cheese
```

1 Spread 2 tablespoons beans over each tortilla. Layer with spinach and ham; sprinkle with egg and cheeses. Roll up tightly; wrap in plastic wrap.

2 Refrigerate for at least 1 hour. Unwrap pinwheels and cut each into six slices.

star sandwiches

PREP/TOTAL TIME: 25 min. | **YIELD:** 8 sandwiches.

A savory egg salad filling makes these star-shaped bites a hit at any buffet or potluck. I prefer yellow egg bread, but feel free to use any bread of your choice.

PAM LANCASTER, WILLIS, VIRGINIA

```
  4  hard-cooked eggs, diced
1/2  cup mayonnaise
  1  teaspoon Dijon mustard
1/4  teaspoon dill weed
```

```
1/8  teaspoon salt
1/8  teaspoon pepper
 16  slices egg bread or white bread
```

1 In a small bowl, combine the eggs, mayonnaise, mustard, dill, salt and pepper. Using a large star-shaped cookie cutter, cut out 16 stars from bread. Spread half of the slices with the egg salad; top with remaining bread.

calla lily tea sandwiches

PREP: 40 min. + chilling | **YIELD:** 1-1/2 dozen.

Your appetizer tray will bloom with beauty when you include these novel lily-shaped sandwiches. The tasty filling will delight guests at your next luncheon or shower.

LEANN WILLIAMS, BEAVERTON, OREGON

```
1/4  cup mayonnaise
  1  teaspoon grated onion
1/4  teaspoon dried tarragon
1/8  teaspoon pepper
  1  can (4-1/2 ounces) chunk white chicken, drained
  1  celery rib, finely chopped
 18  slices white bread, crusts removed
  2  tablespoons butter, softened
  1  tablespoon minced fresh parsley
 18  pieces (1 inch each) julienned carrot
```

1 In a large bowl, combine the first four ingredients; stir in chicken and celery; set aside. With a rolling pin, flatten each slice of bread to 1/8-in. thickness; cut into 2-1/2-in. squares. Spread with butter. Roll up into a funnel shape, overlapping the two adjacent sides; secure with a toothpick.

2 Spoon about 1 teaspoon chicken filling into each sandwich. Cover with plastic wrap; refrigerate for 1 hour.

3 Remove toothpicks. Sprinkle sandwiches with parsley. For the spadix, insert a carrot piece in the center of each lily.

smoked salmon appetizer crepes

PREP: 15 min. + chilling | **COOK:** 5 min. | **YIELD:** 20 appetizers.

A splash of brandy adds impeccable flavor to a creamy filling tucked inside golden, tender crepes. Folded into quarters and cut in half, these charming nibblers are ideal for an elegant dinner party with friends.

KAREN SUE GARBACK-PRISTERA, ALBANY, NEW YORK

- 1   cup milk
- 2   eggs
- 2   egg yolks
- 2   tablespoons butter, melted
- 2   tablespoons brandy *or* unsweetened apple juice
- 1   cup all-purpose flour
- 1/2 teaspoon salt

FILLING:

- 2   packages (3 ounces *each*) cream cheese, softened
- 3   tablespoons heavy whipping cream
- 4   teaspoons minced chives
- 1   package (4 ounces) smoked salmon *or* lox

1   In a small bowl, combine the first five ingredients. Add flour and salt; mix well. Cover and refrigerate for 1 hour.

2   Heat a lightly greased 8-in. nonstick skillet over medium heat; pour 3 tablespoons batter into the center of skillet. Lift and tilt pan to coat bottom evenly. Cook until top appears dry; turn and cook 15-20 seconds longer.

3   Remove to a wire rack. Repeat with remaining batter, greasing skillet as needed. When cool, stack crepes with waxed paper or paper towels in between.

4   For filling, in a large bowl, beat the cream cheese, cream and chives until fluffy. Stir in salmon.

5   To serve, spread each crepe with about 2 tablespoons of the filling. Fold the crepes into quarters; cut each folded crepe into two wedges.

beef-stuffed crescents

PREP: 25 min. | **BAKE:** 15 min. | **YIELD:** 2 dozen.

These hand-held bundles are easy to make and require only six ingredients. I've made them for potlucks and family gatherings—and I never have leftovers!

JENNIFER BUMGARNER, TOPEKA, KANSAS

- 1   pound lean ground beef (90% lean)
- 1   can (4 ounces) chopped green chilies
- 1   package (8 ounces) cream cheese, cubed
- 1/4 teaspoon ground cumin
- 1/4 teaspoon chili powder
- 3   tubes (8 ounces *each*) refrigerated crescent rolls

1   In a large skillet, cook beef and chilies over medium heat until meat is no longer pink; drain. Add the cream cheese, cumin and chili powder. Cool slightly.

2   Separate crescent dough into 24 triangles. Place 1 tablespoon of beef mixture along the short end of each triangle; carefully roll up triangle.

3   Place point side down 2 in. apart on ungreased baking sheets. Bake at 375° for 11-14 minutes or until golden brown. Serve the crescents warm.

mini chicken salad croissants

PREP: 20 min. + chilling | **YIELD:** 20 sandwiches.

This fresh-tasting chicken salad is great for any get-together and could also be served on lettuce or a slice of cantaloupe or honeydew. I substitute halved red seedless grapes for the peppers when I know there will be kids in the crowd. PATRICIA TJUGUM, TOMAHAWK, WISCONSIN

- 1/3 cup sour cream
- 1/3 cup mayonnaise
- 4 teaspoons lemon juice
- 1 teaspoon salt
- 1/4 teaspoon pepper
- 3 cups cubed cooked chicken
- 4 celery ribs, thinly sliced
- 1 cup chopped fresh mushrooms
- 1/4 cup chopped green pepper
- 1/4 cup chopped sweet red pepper
- 4 bacon strips, cooked and crumbled
- 1/2 cup chopped pecans, toasted
- 20 lettuce leaves
- 20 miniature croissants, split

1 In a small bowl, combine the sour cream, mayonnaise, lemon juice, salt and pepper. In a large bowl, combine the chicken, celery, mushrooms and peppers; stir in sour cream mixture until combined. Cover and refrigerate for at least 4 hours.

2 Just before serving, stir in bacon and pecans. Spoon 1/4 cup chicken salad onto each lettuce-lined croissant.

crab salad tea sandwiches

PREP: 1 hour | **YIELD:** 4 dozen.

I make these delightful sandwiches for special occasions. I received the recipe from a friend who served them at her daughter's wedding. They are so delicious, you can't stop at just one! EDIE DESPAIN, LOGAN, UTAH

- 4 celery ribs, finely chopped
- 2 cups reduced-fat mayonnaise
- 4 green onions, chopped
- 1/4 cup lime juice
- 1/4 cup chili sauce
- 1/2 teaspoon seasoned salt
- 8 cups cooked fresh *or* canned crabmeat
- 6 hard-cooked eggs, chopped
- 48 slices whole wheat bread
- 1/2 cup butter, softened
- 48 lettuce leaves
- 1/2 teaspoon paprika

Green onions, cut into thin strips, optional

1 In a large bowl, combine the first six ingredients; gently stir in crab and eggs. Refrigerate.

2 With a 3-in. round cookie cutter, cut a circle from each slice of bread. Spread each with 1/2 teaspoon butter. Top with lettuce and 2 rounded tablespoonfuls of crab salad; sprinkle with paprika. Garnish with onion strips if desired.

tip When peeling the eggshells from hard-cooked eggs, pour off the water as soon as the boiling is done and pour ice water or crushed ice onto the eggs. The shells should peel off easily without sticking.

mini chimichangas

PREP: 1 hour | **COOK:** 15 min. | **YIELD:** 14 servings.

These tasty little bites feature a tantalizing south-of-the-border flavor. They make great party appetizers.

KATHY ROGERS, HUDSON, OHIO

- 1 pound lean ground beef (90% lean)
- 1 medium onion, chopped
- 1 envelope taco seasoning
- 3/4 cup water
- 3 cups (12 ounces) shredded Monterey Jack cheese
- 1 cup (8 ounces) sour cream
- 1 can (4 ounces) chopped green chilies, drained
- 1 package (1 pound) egg roll wrappers (14 count)
- 1 egg white, lightly beaten

Oil for deep-fat frying

Salsa and additional sour cream

1 In a large skillet, cook beef and onion over medium heat until meat is no longer pink; drain. Stir in taco seasoning and water. Bring to a boil. Reduce heat; simmer, uncovered, for 5 minutes, stirring occasionally. Remove from the heat; cool slightly.

2 In a large bowl, combine the cheese, sour cream and chilies. Stir in beef mixture. Place an egg roll wrapper on work surface with one point facing you. Place 1/3 cup filling in center. Fold bottom third or wrapper over filling; fold in sides.

3 Brush top point with egg white; roll up to seal. Repeat with remaining wrappers and filling. (Keep remaining egg roll wrappers covered with waxed paper to avoid drying out.)

4 In a large saucepan, heat 1 in. of oil to 375°. Fry chimichangas for 1-1/2 minutes on each side or until golden brown. Drain on paper towels. Serve warm with salsa and sour cream.

mini subs

PREP/TOTAL TIME: 10 min. | **YIELD:** 4 servings.

One day I was out of bread, so I decided to make my daughter a small sandwich using a hot dog bun instead. She loved that there was no crust!

MELISSA TATUM, GREENSBORO, NORTH CAROLINA

- 3 tablespoons mayonnaise
- 4 hot dog buns, split
- 4 slices process American cheese
- 1/4 pound sliced deli ham
- 1/4 pound sliced deli turkey
- 4 slices tomato, halved
- 1 cup shredded lettuce

1 Spread mayonnaise over cut side of bun bottoms. Layer with cheese, ham, turkey, tomato and lettuce; replace bun tops.

pbj on a stick

PREP/TOTAL TIME: 10 min. | **YIELD:** 4 skewers.

This is a fun take on the classic peanut butter and jelly sandwich. My friends and I love snacking on these when they come to visit. SARA MARTIN, BROOKFIELD, WISCONSIN

- 2 peanut butter and jelly sandwiches
- 4 wooden skewers (5 to 6 inches)
- 1 cup seedless red or green grapes
- 1 small banana, sliced

1 Cut sandwiches into 1-in. squares. For each skewer, thread a grape, sandwich square and banana slice. Add another sandwich square and grape to each. Serve immediately.

FRUIT-FILLED FRENCH TOAST WRAPS, PG. 17

breakfast sandwiches

BREAKFAST QUESADILLAS, PG. 20

HAM & CHEESE BREAKFAST STRUDELS, PG. 19

scrambled egg wraps

PREP/TOTAL TIME: 20 min. | **YIELD:** 6 servings.

My classic wraps will fill your family up with protein and nutrient-rich veggies. Try using flavored wraps or add a little salsa on top to jazz things up.

JANE SHAPTON, IRVINE, CALIFORNIA

- 1 medium sweet red pepper, chopped
- 1 medium green pepper, chopped
- 2 teaspoons canola oil
- 5 plum tomatoes, seeded and chopped
- 6 eggs
- 1/2 cup soy milk
- 1/4 teaspoon salt
- 6 flour tortillas (8 inches), warmed

1 In a large nonstick skillet, saute peppers in oil until tender. Add tomatoes; saute 1-2 minutes longer.

2 Meanwhile, in a large bowl, whisk the eggs, soy milk and salt. Reduce heat to medium; add egg mixture to skillet. Cook and stir until eggs are completely set. Spoon 2/3 cup mixture down the center of each tortilla; roll up.

chocolate french toast

PREP/TOTAL TIME: 15 min. | **YIELD:** 6 servings.

Try this yummy treat for a special breakfast or brunch. Kids go crazy for the hidden chocolate layer!

PAT HABIGER, SPEARVILLE, KANSAS

- 3 eggs
- 1 cup milk
- 1 teaspoon sugar
- 1 teaspoon vanilla extract
- 1/4 teaspoon salt
- 12 slices day-old bread, crusts removed
- 3 milk chocolate candy bars (1.55 ounces *each*), halved
- 2 tablespoons butter

Confectioners' sugar

1 In a large bowl, whisk the eggs, milk, sugar, vanilla and salt. Pour half into an ungreased 13-in. x 9-in. baking dish. Arrange six slices of bread in a single layer over egg mixture. Place one piece of chocolate in the center of each piece of bread. Top with remaining bread; pour remaining egg mixture over all. Let stand for 5 minutes.

2 In a large nonstick skillet, melt butter over medium heat. Toast sandwiches until golden brown on both sides. Dust with confectioners' sugar. Cut sandwiches diagonally; serve warm.

egg salad english muffins

PREP/TOTAL TIME: 15 min. | **YIELD:** 2 servings.

These toasty breakfast muffins help you get a jump start on busy mornings. I make the egg salad ahead of time, then assemble the sandwiches as needed. They're also good with regular bacon or ham. DEBORAH FLORA, SAWYER, KANSAS

- 3 hard-cooked eggs
- 1/4 cup mayonnaise
- 1/4 teaspoon prepared mustard
- 2 English muffins, split and toasted
- 4 slices Canadian bacon
- 1/4 cup shredded cheddar cheese

1 In a small bowl, combine the eggs, mayonnaise and mustard. Place English muffins cut side up on an ungreased baking sheet. Top each with a slice of Canadian bacon, 1/4 cup egg mixture and cheddar cheese.

2 Bake at 350° for 6-8 minutes or until cheese is melted.

dad's quick bagel omelet sandwich

PREP/TOTAL TIME: 20 min. | **YIELD:** 4 servings.

I'm in charge of breakfast at our house. To keep things simple and fun, I wrap these sandwiches in foil and hand them out to my kids as they run out the door for the bus.

ANDREW NODOLSKI, WILLIAMSTOWN, NEW JERSEY

- 1/4 cup finely chopped onion
- 1 tablespoon butter
- 4 eggs
- 1/4 cup chopped tomato
- 1/8 teaspoon salt
- 1/8 teaspoon hot pepper sauce
- 4 slices Canadian bacon
- 4 plain bagels, split
- 4 slices process American cheese

1 In a large skillet, saute onion in butter until tender. Whisk the eggs, tomato, salt and pepper sauce. Add egg mixture to skillet (mixture should set immediately at edges).

2 As the eggs set, push the cooked edges toward the center, letting uncooked portion flow underneath. Cook until eggs are set. Meanwhile, heat bacon in the microwave and toast bagels.

3 Layer bagel bottoms with cheese. Cut omelet into fourths and serve on bagels with bacon.

ham 'n' cheese brunch strips

PREP/TOTAL TIME: 20 min. | **YIELD:** 4 servings.

Do your kids like French toast sticks? Then they're sure to love these tasty brunch strips that boast the same hand-held appeal. TASTE OF HOME TEST KITCHEN

- 2 tablespoons Dijon mustard
- 8 slices white bread, crusts removed
- 8 slices Swiss cheese
- 4 thin slices deli ham
- 2 tablespoons butter, softened

1 Spread mustard over four slices of bread. Layer each with a slice of cheese, ham and another cheese slice. Top with the remaining bread.

2 Butter outside of sandwiches. In a skillet over medium heat, toast sandwiches for 3-4 minutes on each side or until bread is lightly browned and cheese is melted. Remove to a cutting board; cut each sandwich lengthwise into thirds.

berry cream pancakes

PREP/TOTAL TIME: 25 min. | **YIELD:** 8-10 filled pancakes.

Who says pancakes have to be flat? These rolled delights boasting a luscious berry and cream filling are over-the-top indulgent! They can be eaten by hand or savored slowly with a fork. TASTE OF HOME TEST KITCHEN

- 1 cup all-purpose flour
- 1 teaspoon sugar
- 3/4 teaspoon baking powder
- 1/2 teaspoon salt
- 1 egg
- 1 cup buttermilk
- 1 tablespoon butter, melted

CREAM FILLING:

- 1 package (8 ounces) cream cheese, softened
- 3/4 cup confectioners' sugar
- 1/2 teaspoon vanilla extract
- 3 cups sliced fresh strawberries

1 In a large bowl, combine the flour, sugar, baking powder and salt. In another bowl, whisk the egg, buttermilk and butter. Stir into the dry ingredients just until moistened.

2 Pour batter by 1/3 cupfuls onto a greased hot griddle. Turn when bubbles form on top of pancakes; cook until second side is golden brown.

3 Meanwhile, in a small bowl, beat cream cheese, confectioners' sugar and vanilla until smooth. Spread down the center of each pancake; top with strawberries. Fold pancake over filling.

breakfast biscuits 'n' eggs

PREP/TOTAL TIME: 15 min. | **YIELD:** 4 biscuits.

These classic sandwiches are great with freshly baked biscuits or even prebaked ones from the freezer. They're quick to make and a great way to start the day off right.

TERESA HUFF, NEVADA, MISSOURI

- 4 individually frozen biscuits
- 2 teaspoons butter
- 4 eggs
- 4 slices process American cheese
- 4 thin slices deli ham

1 Prepare biscuits according to package directions. Meanwhile, in a large skillet, heat butter until hot. Add eggs; reduce heat to low. Fry until whites are completely set and yolks begin to thicken but are not hard.

2 Split the biscuits. Layer the bottom of each biscuit with cheese, ham and an egg; replace top. Microwave, uncovered, for 30-45 seconds or until cheese is melted.

EDITOR'S NOTE: This recipe was tested in a 1,100-watt microwave.

tip For biscuits to bake properly, arrange your oven rack so that the baking sheet is in the center of the oven. Be sure to use a hot oven (425°-450°) and bake 10-12 minutes for standard-size biscuits. Insulated baking sheets will not allow the bottom of biscuits to brown like regular baking sheets do.

bistro breakfast panini

PREP/TOTAL TIME: 25 min. | **YIELD:** 2 servings.

Love panini sandwiches but don't want to drop a fortune at a bistro or cafe? Try my mouthwatering recipe for this eye-opening creation you can make right in the comfort of your own kitchen. KATHY HARDING, RICHMOND, MISSOURI

6 bacon strips
1 teaspoon butter
4 eggs, lightly beaten
4 slices sourdough bread (3/4 inch thick)
1/8 teaspoon salt
1/8 teaspoon pepper
3 ounces Brie cheese, thinly sliced
8 thin slices apple
1/2 cup fresh baby spinach
2 tablespoons butter, softened

1 In a large skillet, cook bacon over medium heat until crisp. Remove to paper towels to drain.

2 Meanwhile, heat butter in a large skillet over medium heat. Add eggs; cook and stir until set.

3 Place eggs on two slices of bread; sprinkle with salt and pepper. Layer with cheese, apple, bacon, spinach and remaining bread. Butter outsides of sandwiches.

4 Cook on a panini maker or indoor grill for 3-4 minutes or until bread is browned and cheese is melted.

ham and apricot crepes

PREP: 35 min. + chilling | **BAKE:** 20 min. | **YIELD:** 10 servings.

A sweet apricot sauce nicely complements savory ham in these delicate crepes. CANDY EVAVOLD, SAMAMMISH, WASHINGTON

- 1-1/2 cups milk
- 2 eggs, lightly beaten
- 1 tablespoon butter, melted
- 1 cup all-purpose flour
- 20 thin slices deli ham

SAUCE:
- 1 can (15-1/4 ounces) apricot halves
- 2/3 cup sugar
- 2 tablespoons cornstarch
- 1/8 teaspoon salt
- 2 cans (5-1/2 ounces *each*) apricot nectar
- 2 tablespoons butter
- 2 teaspoons lemon juice

1 In a large bowl, beat the milk, eggs and butter. Add flour and beat until well combined. Cover and refrigerate for 1 hour.

2 Heat a lightly greased 8-in. nonstick skillet; pour 2 tablespoons batter into the center of skillet. Lift and tilt pan to evenly coat bottom. Cook until top appears dry; turn and cook 15-20 seconds longer. Remove to a wire rack. Repeat with remaining batter, greasing skillet as needed. When cool, stack crepes with waxed paper or paper towels in between.

3 Place a ham slice on each crepe; roll up. Place crepes in two greased 13-in. x 9-in. baking dishes. Bake, uncovered, at 350° for 20 minutes.

4 Meanwhile, drain apricots, reserving syrup. Cut apricots into 1/4-in. slices; set aside. In a large saucepan, combine the sugar, cornstarch and salt. Add apricot nectar and reserved syrup; stir until smooth. Bring to a boil; cook and stir for 1-2 minutes or until thickened. Remove from the heat; stir in the butter, lemon juice and apricot slices. Serve with crepes.

fruit-filled french toast wraps

PREP/TOTAL TIME: 25 min. | **YIELD:** 2 servings.

Here's a delicious way to get a fiber boost at breakfast. These wraps are easy to make and pretty enough to serve at a special brunch. DAWN JARVIS, BRECKENRIDGE, MINNESOTA

- 1 egg
- 1/4 cup 2% milk
- 1 teaspoon ground cinnamon
- 1/2 teaspoon ground nutmeg
- 2 whole wheat tortillas (8 inches)
- 2 teaspoons butter
- 2/3 cup sliced fresh strawberries
- 2/3 cup fresh blueberries
- 2/3 cup sliced ripe banana
- 3/4 cup (6 ounces) vanilla yogurt
- 1/4 cup granola
- 1 teaspoon confectioners' sugar

1 In a shallow bowl, whisk the egg, milk, cinnamon and nutmeg. Dip both sides of tortillas in egg mixture. In a nonstick skillet, cook tortillas in butter over medium-high heat for 2 minutes on each side or until golden brown.

2 In a small bowl, combine the berries, banana, yogurt and granola. Spoon down the center of tortillas. Roll up; sprinkle with confectioners' sugar. Serve immediately.

spanish-style brunch wraps

PREP/TOTAL TIME: 25 min. | **YIELD:** 2 servings.

Made with a tapenade (a traditional Spanish spread) or a bruschetta topping, this meatless wrap is a vibrant blend of tastes, colors and textures. ROXANNE CHAN, ALBANY, CALIFORNIA

- 3 eggs
- 1 tablespoon shredded Manchego cheese
- 2 teaspoons minced fresh oregano *or* 1/2 teaspoon dried oregano
- 1/4 teaspoon pepper
- 1 tablespoon chopped green onion
- 1 tablespoon chopped roasted sweet red pepper
- 1-1/2 teaspoons olive oil
- 2 sun-dried tomato tortillas (10 inches), warmed
- 1/4 cup tapenade *or* ripe olive bruschetta topping

TOPPING:
- 1-1/2 teaspoons minced fresh parsley
- 1-1/2 teaspoons lemon juice
- 1-1/2 teaspoons olive oil
- 1 garlic clove, minced
- 1/2 teaspoon capers, drained

1 In a small bowl, whisk the eggs, cheese, oregano and pepper; set aside.

2 In a small skillet over medium heat, cook onion and red pepper in oil until tender. Add egg mixture; cook and stir until eggs are completely set.

3 Spread tortillas with tapenade. Spoon egg mixture off center onto tortillas; roll up tightly. Cut wraps in half. Combine topping ingredients; drizzle over wraps. Serve immediately.

prosciutto egg panini

PREP/TOTAL TIME: 30 min. | **YIELD:** 8 servings.

Try my yummy twist on the usual bacon and egg sandwich. It's a breakfast worth waking up for!
ERIN RENOUF MYLROIE, SANTA CLARA, UTAH

- 3 eggs
- 2 egg whites
- 6 tablespoons fat-free milk
- 1 green onion, thinly sliced
- 1 tablespoon Dijon mustard
- 1 tablespoon maple syrup
- 8 slices sourdough bread
- 8 thin slices prosciutto *or* deli ham
- 1/2 cup shredded sharp cheddar cheese
- 8 teaspoons butter

1 In a small bowl, whisk the eggs, egg whites, milk and onion. Coat a large skillet with cooking spray and place over medium heat. Add egg mixture; cook and stir over medium heat until completely set.

2 Combine mustard and syrup; spread over four bread slices. Layer with scrambled eggs, prosciutto and cheese; top with remaining bread. Butter outsides of sandwiches.

3 Cook on a panini maker or indoor grill for 3-4 minutes or until bread is browned and cheese is melted. Cut each panini in half to serve.

ham & cheese breakfast strudels

PREP: 25 min. | **BAKE:** 15 min. | **YIELD:** 6 servings.

*These strudels will get your morning off to a great
start. Sometimes I assemble them in advance and freeze
individually before baking.* JO GROTH, PLAINFIELD, IOWA

- 3 tablespoons butter, *divided*
- 2 tablespoons all-purpose flour
- 1 cup milk
- 1/3 cup shredded Swiss cheese
- 2 tablespoons grated Parmesan cheese
- 1/4 teaspoon salt
- 5 eggs, lightly beaten
- 1/4 pound ground fully cooked ham (about 3/4 cup)
- 6 sheets phyllo dough
- 1/2 cup butter, melted
- 1/4 cup dry bread crumbs

TOPPING:

- 2 tablespoons grated Parmesan cheese
- 2 tablespoons minced fresh parsley

1 In a small saucepan, melt 2 tablespoons butter. Stir in flour
until smooth; gradually add milk. Bring to a boil; cook and stir for
2 minutes or until thickened. Stir in cheeses and salt. Set aside.

2 In a large nonstick skillet, melt remaining butter over medium
heat. Add eggs to the pan; cook and stir until almost set. Stir in ham
and reserved cheese sauce; heat through. Remove from the heat.

3 Place one sheet of phyllo dough on a work surface. (Keep the
remaining phyllo covered with plastic wrap and a damp towel to
prevent it from drying out.) Brush with melted butter. Sprinkle with
2 teaspoons bread crumbs. Fold in half lengthwise; brush again with
butter. Spoon 1/2 cup filling onto phyllo about 2 in. from a short
side. Fold side and edges over filling and roll up.

4 Brush strudels with butter. Repeat. Place desired number of
strudels on a greased baking sheet; sprinkle each with 1 teaspoon
cheese and 1 teaspoon parsley. Bake at 375° for 10-15 minutes or
until golden brown. Serve immediately.

5 TO FREEZE AND BAKE STRUDELS: Individually wrap uncooked
strudels in waxed paper and foil. Freeze for up to 1 month.
Place 2 in. apart on a greased baking sheet; sprinkle with
cheese and parsley. Bake at 375° for 30-35 minutes or until
golden brown.

french toast supreme

PREP/TOTAL TIME: 15 min. | **YIELD:** 4 servings.

*I often use thick slices of French bread or homemade white
bread when fixing these sandwiches. I served them with
a fresh fruit salad at brunch, and everyone asked for the
recipe. It's easy to double or triple for a hungry crowd.*
ELAINE BONICA, BETHEL, MAINE

- 8 slices Texas toast
- 4 slices Canadian bacon
- 4 slices Monterey Jack cheese
- 1 egg
- 1/2 cup refrigerated French vanilla nondairy creamer
Confectioners' sugar, optional
- 1/4 cup seedless raspberry jam

1 On four slices of toast, place one slice of bacon and one slice
of cheese; top with remaining toast. In a shallow bowl, whisk egg
and creamer. Dip sandwiches into egg mixture.

2 On a hot griddle or large skillet coated with cooking spray, cook
French toast for 2-3 minutes on each side or until golden brown.
Sprinkle with confectioners' sugar if desired. Serve with jam.

breakfast quesadillas

PREP/TOTAL TIME: 20 min. | **YIELD:** 2 servings.

Fluffy eggs and a crispy tortilla make this speedy recipe great for brunch. The mild cheese, onion and bacon offer the perfect mix of flavors.

JENNIFER EVANS, OCEANSIDE, CALIFORNIA

- 3 eggs
- 2 flour tortillas (8 inches)
- 1/2 cup shredded fontina cheese
- 2 bacon strips, cooked and crumbled
- 1 green onion, thinly sliced

Sour cream and salsa, optional

1 In a bowl, whisk the eggs. Coat a large skillet with cooking spray. Add eggs; cook and stir over medium heat until completely set.

2 Place tortillas on a griddle. Spoon eggs over half of each tortilla; sprinkle with cheese, bacon and onion. Fold over and cook over low heat for 1-2 minutes on each side or until cheese is melted. Serve with sour cream and salsa.

caramel cream crepes

PREP: 20 min. + chilling | **COOK:** 15 min. | **YIELD:** 6 servings.

These light crepes with a creamy caramel filling are a cinch to whip up. Take one tender bite, and you'll agree it's like having dessert for breakfast! TASTE OF HOME TEST KITCHEN

- 6 tablespoons fat-free milk
- 6 tablespoons egg substitute
- 1-1/2 teaspoons butter, melted
- 1/2 teaspoon vanilla extract
- 6 tablespoons all-purpose flour
- 6 ounces fat-free cream cheese
- 3 tablespoons plus 6 teaspoons fat-free caramel ice cream topping, *divided*
- 2-1/4 cups reduced-fat whipped topping
- 1-1/2 cups fresh raspberries
- 1/3 cup white wine *or* unsweetened apple juice
- 3 tablespoons sliced almonds, toasted

1 In a blender, combine the milk, egg substitute, butter and vanilla; cover and process until blended. Add the flour; cover and process until blended. Cover and refrigerate for 1 hour.

2 Lightly coat a 6-in. nonstick skillet with cooking spray; heat over medium heat. Pour about 2 tablespoons of batter into center of skillet; lift and tilt pan to evenly coat bottom. Cook until top appears dry and bottom is golden; turn and cook 15-20 seconds longer. Remove to a wire rack. Repeat with remaining batter. Stack cooled crepes with waxed paper or paper towels in between.

3 In a small bowl, beat the cream cheese and 3 tablespoons caramel topping until smooth. Fold in whipped topping. Spoon down the center of each crepe. Drizzle with remaining caramel topping; roll up.

4 In a small microwave-safe bowl, combine raspberries and wine. Microwave on high for 30-60 seconds or until warm. Using a slotted spoon, place berries over crepes. Sprinkle with almonds.

crescent sausage rolls

PREP/TOTAL TIME: 30 min. | **YIELD:** 2 servings.

Loaded with pork sausage and cheese, these golden-brown rolls will make breakfast your favorite meal of the day.

CHERIE DURBIN, HICKORY, NORTH CAROLINA

- 1/3 pound bulk pork sausage, cooked and drained
- 1 teaspoon garlic powder
- 1 teaspoon minced fresh parsley
- 1/2 teaspoon grated Parmesan cheese
- 1/4 teaspoon dried basil
- 1 egg, lightly beaten, *divided*
- 1 tube (4 ounces) refrigerated crescent rolls
- 1/2 cup shredded cheddar cheese

1 In a small bowl, combine the sausage, garlic powder, parsley, Parmesan cheese, basil and 2 tablespoons beaten egg. Unroll crescent dough and separate into two rectangles. Place on an ungreased baking sheet; seal perforations.

2 Spoon the sausage mixture into the center of each rectangle. Sprinkle with cheddar cheese. Roll up from a long side; pinch seam to seal. Brush with remaining egg.

3 Bake at 350° for 15-20 minutes or until golden. Cut into slices; serve warm.

ham 'n' egg breakfast wraps

PREP/TOTAL TIME: 20 min. | **YIELD:** 1 serving.

We raise chickens, so I like to find creative ways to make use of our abundance of farm-fresh eggs. I came up with this recipe for an out-of-the-ordinary morning meal.

KATHRYN MARTIN, QUARRYVILLE, PENNSYLVANIA

- 1-1/2 teaspoons butter
- 1 egg, lightly beaten
- 2 ounces thinly sliced deli ham, chopped
- 1 tablespoon chopped green pepper
- 1 tablespoon chopped onion
- 1 tablespoon salsa
- 1 tablespoon sour cream
- 1 flour tortilla (8 inches), warmed
- 2 tablespoons shredded cheddar cheese

1 In a small skillet, melt butter. Add egg; cook and stir over medium heat until completely set. Add the ham, green pepper, onion and salsa; cook until heated through. Spread sour cream over tortilla. Spoon filling over sour cream and sprinkle with cheese. Fold ends and sides over filling and roll up.

tip The sausage filling in Crescent Sausage Rolls and the ham and egg filling in Ham 'n' Egg Breakfast Wraps would also be delicious spooned warm into pita bread or over toasted English muffins for open-faced sandwiches.

ALOHA BURGERS, PG. 28

hot sandwiches

ITALIAN SAUSAGE SANDWICHES, PG. 33

CHICKEN PESTO CLUBS, PG. 30

grilled vegetable sandwich

PREP: 20 min. + marinating | **GRILL:** 10 min. | **YIELD:** 4 servings.

Meat lovers won't miss a thing, but they will rave about the simply fabulous flavor of this hearty grilled veggie sandwich. It tastes wonderful with the ciabatta bread's crispy crust and light, airy texture.

DIANA TSEPERKAS, HAMDEN, CONNECTICUT

- 1 medium zucchini, thinly sliced lengthwise
- 1 medium sweet red pepper, quartered
- 1 small red onion, cut into 1/2-inch slices
- 1/4 cup prepared Italian salad dressing
- 1 loaf ciabatta bread (14 ounces), halved lengthwise
- 2 tablespoons olive oil
- 1/4 cup reduced-fat mayonnaise
- 1 tablespoon lemon juice
- 2 teaspoons grated lemon peel
- 1 teaspoon minced garlic
- 1/2 cup crumbled feta cheese

1 In a large resealable plastic bag, combine the zucchini, pepper, onion and salad dressing. Seal bag and turn to coat; refrigerate for at least 1 hour. Drain and discard marinade.

2 Brush cut sides of bread with oil; set aside. Place vegetables on grill rack. Grill, covered, over medium heat for 4-5 minutes on each side or until crisp-tender. Remove and keep warm. Grill bread, oil side down, over medium heat for 30-60 seconds or until toasted.

3 In a small bowl, combine the mayonnaise, lemon juice, peel and garlic. Spread over bread bottom; sprinkle with cheese. Top with vegetables and remaining bread. Cut into four slices.

basil burgers

PREP/TOTAL TIME: 30 min. | **YIELD:** 8 servings.

Basil is one of my favorite herbs. It gives these burgers a savory flavor that can't be beat.

JENNIE WILBURN, LONG CREEK, OREGON

- 1/2 cup loosely packed basil leaves, minced
- 1/4 cup minced red onion
- 1/4 cup Italian bread crumbs
- 1/4 cup dry red wine
- 1 to 2 teaspoons garlic salt
- 2 pounds lean ground beef (90% lean)
- 8 slices Monterey Jack cheese, optional
- 8 hamburger buns, split

1 In a large bowl, combine the basil, onion, bread crumbs, wine and garlic salt. Crumble beef over mixture and mix well. Shape into eight patties.

2 Grill, covered, over medium heat for 5-7 minutes on each side or until a meat thermometer reads 160° and juices run clear. Top with cheese if desired. Serve on buns.

pulled pork sandwiches

PREP: 20 min. | **COOK:** 6 hours | **YIELD:** 8 servings.

Pork sirloin roast will turn out moist and tender when it's slowly cooked to perfection. The meat shreds easily, and the cumin and garlic add a terrific flavor. The sourdough bread, chipotle mayonnaise, cheddar cheese and sliced tomatos make it complete.

TIFFANY MARTINEZ, ALISO VIEJO, CALIFORNIA

- 1 boneless pork sirloin roast (2 pounds), trimmed
- 1 cup barbecue sauce
- 1/4 cup chopped onion
- 2 garlic cloves, minced
- 1/2 teaspoon ground cumin
- 1/4 teaspoon salt
- 1/8 teaspoon pepper
- 16 slices sourdough bread
- 1 chipotle pepper in adobo sauce, chopped
- 3/4 cup mayonnaise
- 8 slices cheddar cheese
- 2 plum tomatoes, thinly sliced

1 Place pork in a 3-qt. slow cooker. Combine the barbecue sauce, onion, garlic, cumin, salt and pepper; pour over pork. Cover and cook on low for 6-7 hours or until meat is tender. Remove meat. Shred with two forks and return to slow cooker; heat through.

2 Place bread on an ungreased baking sheet. Broil 4-6 in. from the heat for 2-3 minutes on each side or until golden brown.

3 Meanwhile, in a small bowl, combine chipotle pepper and mayonnaise; spread over toast. Spoon 1/2 cup meat mixture onto each of eight slices of toast. Top with cheese, tomatoes and remaining toast.

barbecued chicken hoagies

PREP/TOTAL TIME: 20 min. | **YIELD:** 2 servings.

The day after we held a backyard barbecue, I combined the leftover shredded chicken and a zesty cheese spread on hoagie rolls. We were astounded at the aroma, texture and flavor. Now we look forward to these next-day delights as much as we do the barbecue!

ERIN RENOUF MYLROIE, SANTA CLARA, UTAH

- 1/2 cup shredded sharp cheddar cheese
- 2 tablespoons chopped roasted sweet red peppers
- 2 tablespoons butter, softened
- 1/4 teaspoon garlic powder
- Dash hot pepper sauce
- 2 hoagie buns, split
- 1 cup shredded cooked chicken
- 1/2 cup barbecue sauce

1 In a small bowl, combine the first five ingredients; spread over buns. Place on a baking sheet. Broil 3-4 in. from the heat for 2-4 minutes or until cheese is melted.

2 Meanwhile, in a small microwave-safe bowl, combine chicken and barbecue sauce. Microwave on high for 2-3 minutes or until heated through. Spread chicken mixture over bun bottoms; replace tops.

open-faced turkey burgers

PREP: 30 min. | **GRILL:** 10 min. | **YIELD:** 2 servings.

Here's an opened-faced burger that's juicy, slightly sweet and good for you to boot. It's great for lunch or a light supper. Folks always comment on the savory pesto sauce.

BARBARA LENTO, HOUSTON, PENNSYLVANIA

   3 garlic cloves, peeled
   3 teaspoons olive oil, *divided*
   2 tablespoons mayonnaise
   1 teaspoon prepared pesto
 1/2 teaspoon Italian seasoning
   2 slices whole wheat bread
4-1/2 teaspoons honey
1-1/2 teaspoons Dijon mustard
 1/4 teaspoon salt
Dash pepper
 1/2 pound lean ground turkey
   2 red lettuce leaves
   2 slices tomato
   2 slices sweet onion

1 Place garlic on a double thickness of heavy-duty foil. Drizzle with 1 teaspoon oil. Wrap foil around garlic. Bake at 425° for 15-20 minutes or until garlic is softened. Cool for 10 minutes.

2 Meanwhile, in a small bowl, combine mayonnaise and pesto; set aside. In another small bowl, combine Italian seasoning and remaining oil; brush over bread. Set aside.

3 Squeeze softened garlic into a large bowl. Add the honey, mustard, salt and pepper. Crumble turkey over mixture and mix well. Shape into two patties. Grill, covered, over medium heat for 5-7 minutes on each side or until no longer pink. Grill bread for 1-2 minutes on each side or until toasted. Top each slice of bread with lettuce, burger, tomato, onion and 1 tablespoon mayonnaise mixture.

ham & apple grilled cheese sandwiches

PREP/TOTAL TIME: 25 min. | **YIELD:** 2 servings.

An ordinary grilled cheese sandwich becomes extraordinary when deli ham, sliced apple and honey-spiked mustard are thrown in to the equation. I guarantee this twist on an old favorite will make you melt!

ERIN RENOUF MYLROIE, SANTA CLARA, UTAH

   2 tablespoons Dijon mustard
   2 tablespoons honey
   4 slices sourdough bread
   4 ounces thinly sliced deli ham
   8 thin slices apple
   1 cup (4 ounces) shredded sharp cheddar cheese
4-1/2 teaspoons butter, softened

1 Combine mustard and honey; spread 2 tablespoons mixture over two bread slices. Layer with ham, apple and cheese. Spread remaining bread with remaining mustard mixture; place on top. Butter outsides of sandwiches.

2 In a small skillet over medium heat, toast sandwiches for 2-3 minutes on each side or until cheese is melted.

singapore satay sandwiches

PREP/TOTAL TIME: 30 min. | **YIELD:** 6 servings.

My grandkids think this shredded chicken is the best thing under a bun. The peanut butter flavor and fresh fruit and veggie toppings make it a fun, packable sandwich for school lunches. DIANE HALFERTY, CORPUS CHRISTI, TEXAS

- 1-1/2 pounds boneless skinless chicken breasts
- 1 teaspoon steak seasoning
- 1 tablespoon canola oil
- 3 tablespoons reduced-fat chunky peanut butter
- 1/4 cup unsweetened apple juice
- 2 tablespoons lime juice
- 2 tablespoons reduced-sodium soy sauce
- 2 teaspoons hot pepper sauce
- 6 kaiser rolls, split
- 2 cups torn romaine
- 1 cup shredded carrots
- 1/2 cup julienned peeled cucumber
- 6 tablespoons unsweetened crushed pineapple

1 Sprinkle chicken on both sides with steak seasoning. In a large skillet, cook chicken in oil for 4-7 minutes on each side or until juices run clear. Transfer to a cutting board and shred.

2 In a large microwave-safe bowl, melt peanut butter. Whisk in the apple juice, lime juice, soy sauce and hot pepper sauce. Add chicken and toss to coat.

3 Spoon 1/2 cup chicken mixture onto roll bottoms; top with romaine, carrots, cucumber and pineapple. Replace roll tops.

EDITOR'S NOTE: This recipe was tested with McCormick's Montreal Steak Seasoning. Look for it in the spice aisle.

reuben grill

PREP/TOTAL TIME: 20 min. | **YIELD:** 2 servings.

After one bite, my father declared this reuben a definite keeper! I think you'll agree that the zippy homemade horseradish sauce makes it stand out from the rest.

KATHLEEN HICKS, KANAB, UTAH

- 1/4 cup sour cream
- 2 tablespoons plus 1-1/2 teaspoons chili sauce
- 2 teaspoons prepared horseradish
- 1 tablespoon butter, softened
- 4 slices caraway rye bread
- 4 slices Swiss cheese (3/4 ounce *each*)
- 1/2 cup sauerkraut, rinsed and well drained
- 1/4 pound thinly sliced deli corned beef *or* pastrami

1 In a small bowl, combine the sour cream, chili sauce and horseradish. Spread butter over one side of each slice of bread. Spread sour cream mixture over unbuttered side of two slices; layer with cheese, sauerkraut and corned beef. Top with remaining bread, buttered side up.

2 In a large skillet, toast sandwiches over medium heat for 2-4 minutes on each side or until bread is lightly browned and cheese is melted.

sailor sandwiches with caesar mayo

PREP: 25 min. | **BROIL:** 10 min. | **YIELD:** 2 servings.

These were inspired by the sandwiches in Patricia Cornwell's detective novels. Don't be fooled by the list of ingredients—the recipe goes together quickly. LESLEY PEW, LYNN, MASSACHUSETTS

- 1/4 cup 2% milk
- 1/4 cup cornmeal
- 2 tablespoons all-purpose flour
- 1 tablespoon grated Parmesan cheese
- 1/2 teaspoon dried oregano
- 1/4 teaspoon garlic powder
- 1/4 teaspoon salt
- 1/4 teaspoon pepper
- 2 cod *or* haddock fillets (6 ounces *each*)
- 1 tablespoon butter, melted

CAESAR MAYO:
- 4 teaspoons grated Parmesan cheese
- 4 teaspoons mayonnaise
- 4 teaspoons olive oil
- 1 tablespoon lemon juice
- 1 tablespoon Worcestershire sauce
- 3/4 teaspoon garlic powder

- 1/2 teaspoon ground mustard
- 1/4 teaspoon hot pepper sauce

SANDWICHES:
- 2 kaiser rolls, split and toasted
- 2 lettuce leaves
- 1 small tomato, thinly sliced
- 2 slices sweet onion

1 Place milk in a shallow bowl. In another shallow bowl, combine the cornmeal, flour, cheese and seasonings. Dip fish in milk, then cornmeal mixture.

2 Place fish on a greased broiler pan; drizzle with butter. Broil 4 in. from the heat for 8-10 minutes or until fish flakes easily with a fork.

3 Combine the mayonnaise ingredients; spread over rolls. On roll bottoms, layer with fish, lettuce, tomato and onion. Replace the tops.

3 Drain and discard pineapple marinade. Place pineapple on grill or under broiler to heat through. Layer with lettuce and onion on bottom of buns. Top with burgers, cheese, pineapple and bacon. Replace tops.

coney dogs

PREP: 10 min. | **COOK:** 40 min. | **YIELD:** 24 servings.

Jazz up hot dogs with this seasoned meat sauce. They're a lot more filling than plain dogs, and everyone will devour them in a hurry. DONNA STERNTHAL, SHARPSVILLE, PENNSYLVANIA

   2 pounds lean ground beef (90% lean)
   3 small onions, chopped
   3 cups water
   1 can (12 ounces) tomato paste
   5 teaspoons chili powder
   2 teaspoons rubbed sage
   2 teaspoons salt
   1 teaspoon pepper
 1/2 teaspoon garlic salt
 1/2 teaspoon dried oregano
 1/4 teaspoon cayenne pepper
  24 hot dogs, cooked
  24 hot dog buns
Shredded cheddar cheese, optional

1 In a Dutch oven, cook beef and onions over medium heat until the meat is no longer pink; drain. Stir in the water, tomato paste and seasonings.

2 Cover and simmer for 30 minutes, stirring occasionally. Serve on hot dogs on buns; sprinkle with cheese if desired.

aloha burgers

PREP/TOTAL TIME: 30 min. | **YIELD:** 4 servings.

I love hamburgers and pineapple, so it just seemed natural to combine the two. Now they're a regular request at my house. The tropical twist is a nice change of pace from the same old boring burger. JOI MCKIM-JONES, WAIKOLOA, HAWAII

   1 can (8 ounces) sliced pineapple
 3/4 cup reduced-sodium teriyaki sauce
   1 pound lean ground beef (90% lean)
   1 large sweet onion, sliced
   1 tablespoon butter
   4 lettuce leaves
   4 sesame seed *or* onion buns, split and toasted
   4 slices Swiss cheese
   4 bacon strips, cooked

1 Drain pineapple juice into a small bowl; add teriyaki sauce. Place 3 tablespoons in a resealable plastic bag. Add pineapple; toss to coat and set aside. Shape beef into four patties; place in an 8-in. square baking dish. Pour the remaining teriyaki sauce mixture over patties; marinate for 5-10 minutes, turning once.

2 Drain and discard the teriyaki marinade. Grill, covered, over medium heat or broil 4 in. from the heat for 6-9 minutes on each side or until a meat thermometer reads 160° and juices run clear. Meanwhile, in a small skillet, saute onion in butter until tender, about 5 minutes; set aside.

breaded turkey sandwiches

PREP/TOTAL TIME: 30 min. | **YIELD:** 4 servings.

My son created this unique sandwich recipe using our Thanksgiving dinner leftovers, and it's now a post-Turkey Day tradition. Try grilling it for an even "meltier" sensation. SHANNON BRAY, MAGNOLIA, TEXAS

- 1 egg
- 1/2 cup milk
- 3/4 cup dry bread crumbs
- 1/2 teaspoon salt
- 1/2 teaspoon dried rosemary, crushed
- 1/2 teaspoon pepper
- 1 pound sliced cooked turkey
- 1/3 cup seedless raspberry jam
- 8 slices sourdough bread, toasted
- 8 slices Swiss cheese

1 In a shallow bowl, whisk egg and milk. In another shallow bowl, combine the bread crumbs, salt, rosemary and pepper. Dip turkey slices in egg mixture, then bread crumb mixture.

2 Transfer to a greased 15-in. x 10-in. x 1-in. baking pan. Bake at 400° for 15-18 minutes or until golden brown, turning once.

3 Spread jam over toast; layer four slices with turkey and cheese. Top with remaining toast.

italian patty melts

PREP/TOTAL TIME: 30 min. | **YIELD:** 4 servings.

End the week on a fun note with this easy-to-serve and easy-to-enjoy sandwich. Either serve these Italian-style burgers as a sandwich or open-faced with extra sauce. TASTE OF HOME TEST KITCHEN

- 1 egg
- 1/2 cup spaghetti sauce, *divided*
- 3 tablespoons seasoned bread crumbs
- 1/4 teaspoon pepper
- 1 pound lean ground beef (90% lean)
- 2 tablespoons butter, melted
- 1/4 teaspoon dried basil
- 1/4 teaspoon dried parsley flakes
- 1/8 teaspoon garlic powder
- 8 slices Italian bread
- 1/2 cup shredded part-skim mozzarella cheese

1 In a large bowl, combine the egg, 1/4 cup spaghetti sauce, bread crumbs and pepper. Crumble beef over mixture and mix well. Shape into four oval patties; set aside.

2 Combine butter and seasonings; brush over both sides of bread. In a large skillet, toast bread until lightly browned; set aside.

3 In the same skillet, cook the patties over medium heat for 4-6 minutes on each side or until no longer pink.

4 Spoon remaining sauce over patties; sprinkle with cheese. Cover and cook for 1 minute or until cheese is melted. Place burgers on four slices of toast; top with remaining toast.

chicken pesto clubs

PREP/TOTAL TIME: 10 min. | **YIELD:** 2 servings.

This colorful sandwich is stuffed with fresh, full-flavored ingredients and sizzles to a crispy golden-brown. It's supper in 10 minutes flat!

TERRI CRANDALL, GARDNERVILLE, NEVADA

- 4 slices ready-to-serve fully cooked bacon
- 4 slices sourdough bread
- 2 tablespoons prepared pesto
- 1 cup ready-to-use grilled chicken breast strips
- 2 slices cheddar cheese
- 1 medium tomato, sliced
- 1 cup fresh arugula *or* baby spinach
- 1 tablespoon olive oil

1 Heat bacon according to package directions. Meanwhile, spread bread slices with pesto. Layer two slices with chicken, cheese, tomato, arugula and bacon; top with remaining bread slice.

2 Brush outsides of sandwiches with oil. Cook on an indoor grill for 3-4 minutes or until bread is browned and cheese is melted.

tip Arugula is a small tender leafy green with a peppery taste. It is often used in salads, alone or as part of a mix of greens, in pizzas, sandwiches and pesto sauces.

cajun burgers

PREP/TOTAL TIME: 20 min. | **YIELD:** 8 servings.

You don't need to hail from the bayous of Louisiana to appreciate these burgers. The onions, garlic, green pepper and spices give it just the right amount of Cajun kick.

RON TREADAWAY, ACWORTH, GEORGIA

- 1 large green pepper, chopped
- 1 large onion, chopped
- 6 green onions, thinly sliced
- 6 garlic cloves, minced
- 1 egg
- 2 tablespoons Worcestershire sauce
- 1 tablespoon dry bread crumbs
- 1 tablespoon soy sauce
- 1 tablespoon cream cheese, softened
- 1/4 teaspoon cornstarch
- 1/4 teaspoon salt
- 1/4 teaspoon pepper
- 1/4 teaspoon seasoned salt
- 1/4 teaspoon dried thyme
- 1/4 teaspoon ground mustard
- 1/4 teaspoon hot pepper sauce
- 2 pounds lean ground beef (90% lean)
- 8 hamburger buns, split

1 In a large bowl, combine the first 16 ingredients. Crumble beef over mixture and mix well. Shape into eight patties.

2 Grill patties over medium heat for 5-7 minutes on each side or until a meat thermometer reads 160° and juices run clear. Serve on buns.

open-faced meatball sandwiches

PREP: 30 min. | **COOK:** 10 min. | **YIELD:** 8 servings.

These scrumptious sandwiches feature tender meatballs prepared with a host of seasonings. Topped with mozzarella cheese, the mouthwatering handhelds will soon be much-requested favorites. KAREN BARTHEL, NORTH CANTON, OHIO

- 1/4 cup egg substitute
- 1/2 cup soft bread crumbs
- 1/4 cup finely chopped onion
- 2 garlic cloves, minced
- 1/2 teaspoon onion powder
- 1/2 teaspoon dried oregano
- 1/2 teaspoon dried basil
- 1/4 teaspoon pepper

Dash salt

- 1-1/4 pounds lean ground turkey
- 2 cups garden-style pasta sauce
- 4 hoagie buns, split
- 2 tablespoons shredded part-skim mozzarella cheese

Shredded Parmesan cheese, optional

1 In a large bowl, combine the first nine ingredients. Crumble turkey over mixture and mix well. Shape into 40 meatballs, 1 in. each. In a large skillet coated with cooking spray, brown meatballs in batches; drain.

2 Place meatballs in a large saucepan. Add the pasta sauce; bring to a boil. Reduce heat; cover and simmer for 10-15 minutes or until meat is no longer pink.

3 Spoon meatballs and sauce onto bun halves; sprinkle with mozzarella cheese and Parmesan cheese if desired.

grilled bacon-tomato sandwiches

PREP/TOTAL TIME: 20 min. | **YIELD:** 2 servings.

My family loves these sandwiches. Fresh basil, tangy Italian dressing and melted cheese meld perfectly together in this simple sandwich. BETTY SNODDY, FRANKLIN, MISSOURI

- 4 slices Italian bread (1/2 inch thick)
- 4 slices provolone cheese (1 ounce *each*)
- 4 slices tomato
- 4 bacon strips, cooked and halved
- 2 teaspoons minced fresh basil *or* 1/2 teaspoon dried basil
- 2 tablespoons Italian salad dressing

1 Top two slices of bread with a slice of cheese; layer with tomato, bacon, basil and remaining cheese. Top with remaining bread. Brush dressing over outsides of sandwiches.

2 In a large skillet over medium heat, toast sandwiches for 2-3 minutes on each side or until cheese is melted.

> **tip** The recipe for Grilled Bacon-Tomato Sandwiches is easy to double or triple if you're serving more than two people. And here's an easy way to toast them all at once: Prepare the sandwiches as you would for the griddle, but place all of them on a cookie sheet instead. Bake in a 350° oven for 5-8 minutes on each side until they are golden brown.

taco burgers

PREP/TOTAL TIME: 25 min. | **YIELD:** 6 servings.

My family loves tacos, but I dislike all the cleanup. So I developed these burgers as a tasty but "neat" alternative.

LINDA LOGAN, WARREN, OHIO

1 cup finely crushed corn chips
1 envelope taco seasoning
1 tablespoon dried minced onion
1 egg, lightly beaten
1-1/2 pounds lean ground beef (90% lean)
6 slices cheddar cheese
Sandwich buns, split
Lettuce leaves
Tomato slices
Salsa, optional

1 In a large bowl, combine the corn chips, taco seasoning, onion and egg. Crumble beef over mixture and mix well. Shape into six patties. Broil or grill until a meat thermometer reads 160° and juices run clear.

2 Top each burger with a slice of cheese; cook just until the cheese begins to melt. Serve burgers on buns with lettuce, tomato and salsa if desired.

italian sausage sandwiches

PREP/TOTAL TIME: 30 min. | **YIELD:** 2 servings.

Give these saucy sandwiches a whirl for a casual but hearty meal. They're full of traditional Italian flavor and ready in a jiffy. TASTE OF HOME TEST KITCHEN

- 2 Italian sausage links (4 ounces *each*)
- 1/4 cup water
- 1 small green pepper, cut into strips
- 1 small onion, halved and thinly sliced
- 1 tablespoon olive oil
- 1 cup spaghetti sauce
- 1/4 teaspoon dried basil
- 2 brat buns, split and toasted
- 2 tablespoons shredded Italian cheese blend

1 Place sausages and water in a large skillet; bring to a boil. Reduce heat; cover and simmer for 10 minutes. Uncover; cook 5-10 minutes longer or until meat is no longer pink; drain. Remove sausages and keep warm.

2 In the same skillet, saute pepper and onion in oil until tender. Return sausages to pan. Stir in spaghetti sauce and basil; heat through. Serve sausages on buns with sauce and cheese.

mustard turkey sandwiches

PREP: 10 min. + marinating | **GRILL:** 10 min. | **YIELD:** 6 servings.

This recipe is perfect for small dinner parties. The turkey can marinate while you visit with guests, then simply pop it onto the grill for a mouthwatering meal in no time.
MONICA WILCOTT, STURGIS, SASKATCHEWAN

- 1/2 cup olive oil
- 1/2 cup honey
- 1/4 cup Dijon mustard
- 1 tablespoon curry powder
- Pinch cayenne pepper
- 1 package (17.6 ounces) turkey breast cutlets
- 6 onion *or* kaiser rolls, split
- Lettuce leaves

1 In a small saucepan, combine the first five ingredients. Cook and stir over medium heat until mixture is combined. Cool slightly; set aside 1/4 cup. Pour remaining mixture into a large resealable plastic bag; add turkey. Seal bag and refrigerate for at least 2 hours.

2 Drain and discard marinade. Grill turkey for 4 minutes on each side or until no longer pink. Spread cut sides of rolls with reserved honey mixture. Add lettuce and turkey.

tip You can easily enhance any sandwich with mouthwatering toppings such as guacamole, salsa, cheese spreads, flavored mayonnaise, Swiss cheese, blue cheese, sauteed mushrooms, tomato slices or strips of crispy bacon.

open-faced cheesesteak sandwiches

PREP/TOTAL TIME: 30 min. | **YIELD:** 2 servings.

You might need a fork to eat this messy, utterly satisfying sandwich. Hot pepper sauce and pepper Jack cheese add a kick to the tender roast beef and veggies.

MICHAEL KLOTZ, SCOTTSDALE, ARIZONA

- 1   French roll, split
- 2   teaspoons butter
- 1/4 teaspoon garlic powder
- 1/2 cup julienned green pepper
- 1/4 cup sliced onion
- 1/4 teaspoon salt
- 1/4 teaspoon pepper
- 2   tablespoons canola oil, *divided*
- 1/3 pound sliced deli roast beef
- 1/2 teaspoon hot pepper sauce
- 4   slices pepper Jack cheese (3/4 ounce *each*)

1   Spread roll halves with butter; sprinkle with garlic powder. Set aside.

2   In a small skillet, saute the green pepper, onion, salt and pepper in 1 tablespoon oil until tender. Remove and keep warm. In the same skillet, saute beef and hot sauce in remaining oil until heated through. Spoon onto buns; top with pepper mixture and cheese.

3   Place on a baking sheet. Broil 2-3 in. from the heat for 2-4 minutes or until cheese is melted.

lasagna in a bun

PREP: 25 min. | **BAKE:** 20 min. | **YIELD:** 8 servings.

This tasty recipe is always a treat because it's a little like traditional lasagna and a little like a sandwich all in one!

MARGARET PETERSON, FOREST CITY, IOWA

- 3/4 pound lean ground beef (90% lean)
- 1   can (14-1/2 ounces) diced tomatoes, drained
- 2   tablespoons onion soup mix
- 1/4 teaspoon dried basil
- 1/4 teaspoon dried oregano
- 8   hoagie buns
- 3/4 cup 4% cottage cheese
- 1   egg, lightly beaten
- 1   cup (4 ounces) shredded part-skim mozzarella cheese, *divided*

1   In a large skillet, cook beef over medium heat until no longer pink; drain. Stir in the tomatoes, soup mix, basil and oregano. Cook, uncovered, for 5 minutes or until heated through.

2   Cut a thin slice off the top of each bun. Carefully hollow out bun bottoms, leaving a 1/4-in. shell (discard removed bread or save for another use).

3   In a small bowl, combine the cottage cheese, egg and 1/4 cup mozzarella cheese; spoon into buns. Top with meat mixture; sprinkle with remaining mozzarella cheese. Replace bun tops.

4   Wrap each sandwich in heavy-duty foil; place on a baking sheet. Bake at 400° for 20-25 minutes or until heated through.

bbq beef sandwiches

PREP: 15 min. | **COOK:** 8 hours | **YIELD:** 14 sandwiches.

After years of searching, I finally found a recipe for shredded barbecued beef that's a hit with everybody. It's easy to freeze for future meals—if there's any left over!

LALAREBECCA ROHLAND, MEDFORD, WISCONSIN

- 2 cups ketchup
- 1 medium onion, chopped
- 1/4 cup cider vinegar
- 1/4 cup molasses
- 2 tablespoons Worcestershire sauce
- 2 garlic cloves, minced
- 1/2 teaspoon salt
- 1/2 teaspoon ground mustard
- 1/2 teaspoon pepper
- 1/4 teaspoon garlic powder
- 1/4 teaspoon crushed red pepper flakes
- 1 boneless beef chuck roast (3 pounds)
- 14 sesame seed hamburger buns, split

1 In a large bowl, combine the first 11 ingredients. Cut roast in half; place in a 5-qt. slow cooker. Pour ketchup mixture over roast. Cover and cook on low for 8-9 hours or until meat is tender.

2 Remove meat and shred with two forks. Skim fat from cooking juices. Return meat to slow cooker; heat through. Using a slotted spoon, serve beef on buns.

game day brats

PREP/TOTAL TIME: 25 min. | **YIELD:** 6 servings.

Looking for a twist on the usual tailgate fare? Add French salad dressing and Monterey Jack cheese to brats to kick the flavor up a notch. Instead of brats, you can also use cooked Italian sausage links with tasty results.

LAURA MCDOWELL, LAKE VILLA, ILLINOIS

- 6 fully cooked bratwurst links (1 to 1-1/4 pounds)
- 3/4 cup sauerkraut, rinsed and well drained
- 6 tablespoons French salad dressing
- 6 tablespoons shredded Monterey Jack cheese
- 6 brat buns, split

1 Make a lengthwise slit three-fourths of the way through each bratwurst to within 1/2 in. of each end. Fill with sauerkraut; top with dressing and cheese.

2 Place the bratwurst in buns; wrap individually in a double thickness of heavy-duty foil (about 12 in. x 10 in.). Grill, covered, over medium-hot heat for 10-15 minutes or until heated through and cheese is melted.

tip When you have leftover bratwurst after a barbecue, slice it up and sprinkle the pieces on top of a frozen pizza before baking. It makes a tasty topper and a nice variation from traditional sausage or pepperoni.

italian blts

PREP/TOTAL TIME: 20 min. | **YIELD:** 2 servings.

The brilliant method of toasting BLTs in a coating of crispy bread crumbs takes these sandwiches from satisfying to spectacular! JOYCE MOUL, YORK HAVEN, PENNSYLVANIA

- 2 turkey bacon strips, diced
- 4 slices Italian bread (1/2 inch thick)
- 2 slices reduced-fat provolone cheese
- 2 lettuce leaves
- 1 small tomato, sliced
- 4 teaspoons fat-free Italian salad dressing
- 1/3 cup panko (Japanese) bread crumbs
- Butter-flavored cooking spray
- 1/2 teaspoon olive oil

1 In a small skillet, cook bacon over medium heat until crisp. Layer two bread slices with cheese, bacon, lettuce and tomato; top with remaining bread.

2 Brush outsides of sandwiches with salad dressing. Place bread crumbs in a shallow bowl. Coat sandwiches with bread crumbs; spray with butter-flavored cooking spray.

3 In a large skillet over medium heat, toast sandwiches in oil for 2-3 minutes on each side or until bread is lightly browned.

sloppy joes for 8 dozen

PREP: 20 min. | **COOK:** 1-1/2 hours | **YIELD:** 96 servings.

In need of an all-star recipe to serve a crowd? Give my hearty sloppy joes a try at your next family picnic or potluck. Any leftovers taste great over rice, biscuits or baked potatoes. WANIETA PENNER, MCPHERSON, KANSAS

- 15 pounds lean ground beef (90% lean)
- 6 medium onions, chopped
- 1 gallon ketchup
- 3/4 cup Worcestershire sauce
- 1/2 cup packed brown sugar
- 1/2 cup prepared yellow mustard
- 1/4 cup white vinegar
- 1 tablespoon chili powder
- 96 hamburger buns, split

1 In two stockpots over medium heat, cook and stir beef and onions until meat is no longer pink; drain.

2 Stir in the ketchup, Worcestershire sauce, brown sugar, mustard, vinegar and chili powder. Bring to a boil. Reduce heat; simmer, uncovered, for 1 hour to allow flavors to blend. Spoon 1/3 cup onto each bun.

stuffed pork burgers

PREP/TOTAL TIME: 30 min. | **YIELD:** 4 servings.

Guests will go hog wild for these stuffed burgers. I've prepared pork in a variety of ways and with a variety of seasonings, but everyone agrees these burgers are the best.

JEAN SMITH, MONONA, IOWA

- 1/2 cup chopped fresh mushrooms
- 1/4 cup sliced green onions
- 1/4 teaspoon garlic powder
- 1 tablespoon butter
- 2 tablespoons Worcestershire sauce
- 1 teaspoon ground mustard
- 1/2 teaspoon salt
- 1/2 teaspoon pepper
- 1-1/2 pounds ground pork
- 4 kaiser rolls, split
- 4 lettuce leaves
- 4 slices red onion
- 8 thin slices tomato

Prepared mustard

1 In a small skillet, saute the mushrooms, onions and garlic powder in butter until the vegetables are tender. Remove from the heat.

2 In a large bowl, combine the Worcestershire sauce, mustard, salt and pepper. Crumble pork over mixture and mix well.

3 Shape into eight patties. Spoon mushroom mixture into the center of four patties to within 1/2-in. of edges. Top with remaining patties; pinch edges to seal.

4 Grill, uncovered, over medium heat for 5-7 minutes on each side or until a meat thermometer reads 160° and meat juices run clear. Serve on rolls with lettuce, onion, tomato and mustard.

open-faced tuna melts

PREP/TOTAL TIME: 25 min. | **YIELD:** 2 servings.

Looking for a tasty way to get your family to eat more fish? Try this light take on classic tuna melts. These simple open-faced sandwiches are an easy way to get your daily dose of healthy omega-3 fatty acids.

ALICE STRAPP-MEISTER, NEW ROSS, NOVA SCOTIA

- 1/4 cup fat-free mayonnaise
- 2 tablespoons chopped green pepper
- 1-1/2 teaspoons chopped onion
- 1-1/2 teaspoons chopped celery
- 1-1/2 teaspoons prepared mustard
- 1/4 teaspoon Worcestershire sauce
- 1 can (6 ounces) tuna, drained and flaked
- 2 hamburger buns, split and toasted
- 4 slices tomato
- 2 tablespoons shredded reduced-fat cheddar cheese

1 In a small bowl, combine the first six ingredients; stir in tuna. Spread over each bun half; top with a tomato slice. Sprinkle with cheese.

2 Place on a baking sheet. Broil 3-4 in. from the heat for 3-5 minutes or until lightly browned and cheese is melted.

tip Not only are Open-Faced Tuna Melts hot and delicious, they're good for you, too. For extra nutrition, add white kidney beans to the tuna mixture to amp up the fiber and serve on whole-wheat buns instead of white.

provolone 'n' turkey sandwiches

PREP/TOTAL TIME: 15 min. | **YIELD:** 2 servings.

Rye bread complements the zippy flavors in this simple, sensational sandwich. If you prefer a milder taste, simply omit the red pepper and substitute regular deli turkey for the peppered. LYNNE MIESS, NEW PORT RICHEY, FLORIDA

- 4 slices rye bread
- 2 teaspoons Dijon mustard
- 4 slices provolone cheese (1/2 ounce *each*)
- 10 spinach leaves
- 4 ounces sliced deli peppered turkey
- 4 roasted sweet red pepper strips
- 4 teaspoons butter

1 Spread two bread slices with mustard. Layer with cheese, spinach, turkey and red pepper. Top with remaining bread. Spread outsides of sandwiches with butter.

2 In a large skillet over medium heat, toast sandwiches for 3 minutes on each side or until cheese is melted.

EDITOR'S NOTE: This recipe was tested with Vlasic roasted red pepper strips.

tip If you enjoy grilled sandwiches, you may want to invest in an electric or stovetop griddle. Not only can you grill four to six sandwiches at a time, but you can also fry up bacon, sliced onions and other warm sandwich toppings.

chipotle bbq pork sandwiches

PREP: 20 min. | **GRILL:** 20 min. | **YIELD:** 4 servings.

I made these for a summer picnic with guests who love traditional barbecued pork sandwiches but wanted something lighter. They loved these and didn't miss the extra calories one bit. The crunchy coleslaw on top helps tame the heat. PRISCILLA YEE, CONCORD, CALIFORNIA

- 1/2 cup barbecue sauce
- 1 tablespoon honey
- 2 chipotle peppers in adobo sauce, chopped
- 1 pork tenderloin (1 pound)
- 1-1/2 cups coleslaw mix
- 2 tablespoons reduced-fat sour cream
- 2 tablespoons Miracle Whip Light
- 1 tablespoon Dijon mustard
- 4 hamburger buns, split

1 In a small bowl, combine the barbecue sauce, honey and peppers. Set aside 1/4 cup until serving.

2 Moisten a paper towel with cooking oil; using long-handled tongs, lightly coat the grill rack. Prepare grill for indirect heat, using a drip pan.

3 Place pork over drip pan and grill, covered, over indirect medium-hot heat for 20-25 minutes or until a meat thermometer reads 160°, basting occasionally with remaining barbecue sauce. Let stand for 5 minutes before slicing.

4 Meanwhile, combine the coleslaw mix, sour cream, Miracle Whip Light and mustard. Brush cut sides of buns with reserved barbecue sauce. Cut pork into 1/4-in. slices; place on bun bottoms. Top with coleslaw and bun tops.

waffled monte cristos

PREP/TOTAL TIME: 25 min. | **YIELD:** 2 servings.

My husband and I enjoy Monte Cristos so much that I created this non-fried version to cut down on fat. The addition of orange peel and pecans makes these hot, oozing sandwiches absolutely delicious! MARY SHIVERS, ADA, OKLAHOMA

- 1 egg
- 1/4 cup 2% milk
- 1 teaspoon sugar
- 1 teaspoon grated orange peel
- 4 slices white bread
- 2 tablespoons finely chopped pecans
- 4 slices process American cheese (2/3 ounce *each*)
- 2 thin slices deli turkey (1/2 ounce *each*)
- 2 slices Swiss cheese (3/4 ounce *each*)
- 2 thin slices deli ham (1/2 ounce *each*)
- 2 teaspoons butter
- 2 teaspoons confectioners' sugar
- 1/4 cup seedless raspberry jam

1 In a shallow bowl, combine the egg, milk, sugar and orange peel. Dip bread into egg mixture. Place on a preheated waffle iron; sprinkle each slice of bread with pecans. Bake according to manufacturer's directions until golden brown.

2 Place an American cheese slice on two bread slices; layer with the turkey, Swiss cheese, ham and remaining American cheese. Top with remaining bread; butter outsides of sandwiches.

3 Toast sandwiches in a skillet for 1-2 minutes on each side or until cheese is melted. Dust with confectioners' sugar; serve with jam.

freezer veggie burgers

PREP: 25 min. + freezing | **BAKE:** 30 min. | **YIELD:** 6 servings.

These veggie burgers make a fantastic low-cholesterol alternative to beef burgers. Make them at your convenience and store in the freezer until you need a fast bite on a busy night. ELAINE SOLOCHIER, CONCORD, NORTH CAROLINA

- 1 can (16 ounces) kidney beans, rinsed and drained
- 1/2 cup old-fashioned oats
- 2 tablespoons ketchup
- 1/2 cup finely chopped fresh mushrooms
- 1 medium onion, finely chopped
- 1 medium carrot, shredded
- 1 small sweet red pepper, finely chopped
- 2 garlic cloves, minced
- 1/2 teaspoon salt
- 1/8 teaspoon white pepper
- 6 hamburger buns, split
- 6 lettuce leaves
- 6 slices tomato

1 Place the beans, oats and ketchup in a food processor; cover and pulse until blended. Transfer to a small bowl; stir in the vegetables, garlic and seasonings. Shape into six 3-in. patties; wrap each in plastic wrap and freeze.

2 When ready to use, unwrap burgers and place on a baking sheet coated with cooking spray. Bake at 350° for 30 minutes or until heated through, turning once. Serve on buns with lettuce and tomato.

tex-mex beef sandwiches

PREP: 25 min. | **COOK:** 8 hours | **YIELD:** 8 servings.

Everyone loves these hearty Southwestern sandwiches. Cocoa adds depth to the flavor. It's hard to identify, so guests are often surprised when I reveal the secret ingredient. BRENDA THEISEN, ADDISON, MICHIGAN

- 1 boneless beef chuck roast (3 pounds)
- 1 envelope burrito seasoning
- 2 tablespoons baking cocoa
- 1 large green pepper, coarsely chopped
- 1 large sweet red pepper, coarsely chopped
- 1 large onion, chopped
- 1 cup beef broth
- 1/2 cup ketchup
- 8 hoagie buns, split

1 Cut roast in half. Combine burrito seasoning and cocoa; rub over meat. Place peppers and onion in a 3- or 4-qt. slow cooker; top with meat. Combine broth and ketchup; pour over meat.

2 Cover and cook on low for 8-10 hours or until meat is tender. Skim fat. When cool enough to handle, shred meat with two forks and return to slow cooker; heat through. Using a slotted spoon, spoon 1/2 cup onto each bun.

tip To easily chop bell peppers, hold the pepper by the stem and slice from the top of the pepper down. Use this technique to slice around the seeds when a recipe calls for chopped or julienned peppers.

pork tenderloin panini with fig port jam

PREP: 1 hour | **COOK:** 5 min. | **YIELD:** 4 servings.

I make these sophisticated yet simple sandwiches for a special dinner with my sweetheart, or I sometimes cut them into smaller pieces to serve as appetizers at parties. They're great hot or cold, but if serving cold, add the watercress for extra color. CASEY GALLOWAY, COLUMBIA, MISSOURI

- 1/3 cup port wine *or* grape juice
- 2 tablespoons water
- 2 dried figs, chopped
- 1 fresh rosemary sprig
- 1 tablespoon honey
- 1/8 teaspoon salt

Dash pepper

SANDWICHES:

- 1 pork tenderloin (3/4 pound)
- 1/4 teaspoon salt
- 1/4 teaspoon pepper
- 8 slices sourdough bread
- 1/4 cup crumbled goat cheese
- 1 cup watercress, optional

Cooking spray

1 For jam, in small saucepan, combine the first seven ingredients. Bring to a boil. Reduce heat; simmer, uncovered, until liquid is reduced to about 1/4 cup, about 15 minutes.

2 Remove from the heat. Cool slightly; discard rosemary. Transfer mixture to blender; cover and process until blended. Cover and chill until serving.

3 Meanwhile, sprinkle tenderloin with salt and pepper; place on a rack in a shallow roasting pan. Bake, uncovered, at 350° for 40-50 minutes or until a meat thermometer reads 160°. Let stand for 10 minutes before slicing. Cut pork into 1/8-in. slices.

4 On four bread slices, layer the pork, jam, cheese and watercress if desired; top with remaining bread. Coat outsides of sandwiches with cooking spray.

5 Cook on a panini maker or indoor grill for 3-4 minutes or until bread is lightly browned.

french dip sandwiches

PREP/TOTAL TIME: 15 min. | **YIELD:** 4 servings.

Treat yourself or a loved one to a restaurant-quality lunch with this classic. The flavorful au jus is a snap to prepare.
CAROLE LANTHIER, COURTICE, ONTARIO

- 1 pound sliced deli roast beef
- 1 can (10-1/2 ounces) condensed beef broth, undiluted
- 1/2 cup steak sauce, *divided*
- 1 tablespoon Dijon mustard
- 4 French rolls, split

1 In a 1-1/2-qt. microwave-safe bowl, combine the beef, broth and 1/4 cup steak sauce. Cover and microwave on high for 2-3 minutes or until heated through.

2 Meanwhile, combine mustard and remaining steak sauce; spread over roll bottoms. Using a slotted spoon, place beef on rolls; replace tops. Serve with broth mixture for dipping.

EDITOR'S NOTE: This recipe was tested in a 1,100-watt microwave.

BISTRO TURKEY SANDWICHES, PG. 51

cold sandwiches

SPINACH FETA CROISSANTS FOR 2, PG. 48

CREAMY BEEF SANDWICHES, PG. 53

turkey focaccia club

PREP/TOTAL TIME: 20 min. | **YIELD:** 4 servings.

Homemade cranberry-pecan mayo makes this sandwich pure heaven. It's delicious the day after Thanksgiving or any day of the year. JUDY WILSON, SUN CITY WEST, ARIZONA

CRANBERRY PECAN MAYONNAISE:
- 1/2 cup mayonnaise
- 1/2 cup whole-berry cranberry sauce
- 2 tablespoons Dijon mustard
- 2 tablespoons chopped pecans, toasted
- 1 tablespoon honey

SANDWICH:
- 1 loaf (8 ounces) focaccia bread
- 3 lettuce leaves
- 1/2 pound thinly sliced cooked turkey
- 1/4 pound sliced Gouda cheese
- 8 slices tomato
- 6 bacon strips, cooked

1 In a small bowl, combine the mayonnaise, cranberry sauce, mustard, pecans and honey.

2 Cut bread in half horizontally; spread with cranberry pecan mayonnaise. Layer with lettuce, turkey, cheese, tomato and bacon; replace bread top. Cut into wedges.

sunny blt sandwiches

PREP/TOTAL TIME: 20 min. | **YIELD:** 2 servings.

Smoky bacon, ripe tomatoes and crisp lettuce are fantastic on their own, but even better when layered with my creamy homemade egg salad. This lunchtime creation is destined to become one of your all-time favorites.
KELLY MCDONALD, EDINBURG, TEXAS

- 4 bacon strips
- 4 hard-cooked eggs, chopped
- 2 tablespoons 4% cottage cheese
- 1 tablespoon cream cheese, softened
- 2 teaspoons sweet pickle juice
- 1/2 teaspoon prepared mustard
- 1/4 teaspoon onion powder
- 1/8 teaspoon salt
- 1/8 teaspoon pepper
- 1/8 teaspoon Worcestershire sauce
- 4 slices whole wheat bread, toasted
- 2 lettuce leaves
- 2 slices tomato
- 2 slices Swiss cheese (3/4 ounce *each*)

1 In a large skillet, cook bacon over medium heat until crisp. Remove to paper towels to drain.

2 In a large bowl, combine the eggs, cottage cheese, cream cheese, pickle juice, mustard, onion powder, salt, pepper and Worcestershire sauce. On two slices of toast, layer the lettuce, tomato, cheese slices and bacon. Top with egg salad and remaining toast.

curried beef sandwiches

PREP/TOTAL TIME: 10 min. | **YIELD:** 6 sandwiches.

Classic roast beef takes on a whole new meaning when combined with my special chutney and curry mayonnaise.

TASTE OF HOME TEST KITCHEN

- 1/3 cup mayonnaise
- 1/4 cup chutney
- 1/4 teaspoon curry powder
- 12 slices whole wheat bread
- 1-1/4 pounds thinly sliced deli roast beef
- 6 lettuce leaves
- 6 tomato slices

1 In a small bowl, combine the mayonnaise, chutney and curry. Spread about 1 tablespoon over six slices of bread; layer with beef, lettuce and tomato. Top with remaining bread.

nutty marmalade sandwiches

PREP: 10 min. + freezing | **YIELD:** 3 servings.

I make dozens of these fun-filled sandwiches to freeze for a few weeks' worth of brown-bag lunches. They taste so fresh you would never know they were ever frozen. The sweet marmalade flavor is what makes them so good.

IOLA EGLE, BELLA VISTA, ARKANSAS

- 1/2 cup peanut butter
- 1/4 cup orange marmalade
- 1/4 cup shredded sharp cheddar cheese
- 1 to 2 teaspoons lemon juice
- 6 slices bread

1 In a small bowl, combine the peanut butter, marmalade, cheese and lemon juice. Spread over three slices of bread; top with remaining bread.

2 Freeze for up to 4 months. Remove from the freezer at least 4 hours before serving.

ham salad croissants

PREP/TOTAL TIME: 30 min. | **YIELD:** 8 servings.

Folks always enjoy this crunchy, full-flavored ham salad. It's always welcome at church dinners and family gatherings, and it's a great way to use leftover ham.

JO RILEY, HART, TEXAS

- 3 cups ground fully cooked ham
- 2 cups (8 ounces) shredded cheddar cheese
- 2 celery ribs, finely chopped
- 8 green onions, chopped
- 1/3 cup unsalted sunflower kernels
- 1/3 cup finely chopped green pepper
- 1/3 cup chopped dill pickle
- 1/3 cup mayonnaise
- 1/3 cup sour cream
- 1 jar (4 ounces) diced pimientos, drained
- 1 teaspoon ranch salad dressing mix
- 1 teaspoon coarsely ground pepper
- 1 teaspoon minced fresh parsley
- 8 lettuce leaves
- 8 croissants, split

1 In a large bowl, combine the first seven ingredients. In a small bowl, combine the mayonnaise, sour cream, pimientos, salad dressing mix, pepper and parsley. Pour over ham mixture; toss to coat. Serve on lettuce-lined croissants.

simon's famous tuna salad

PREP/TOTAL TIME: 15 min. | **YIELD:** 5 servings.

This nicely seasoned tuna salad makes a simple and delicious lunch. Crunchy carrots lend a unique texture and flavor. SIMON SEITZ, HIGHLAND, NEW YORK

- 3 cans (6 ounces *each*) light water-packed tuna, drained and flaked
- 3/4 cup fat-free mayonnaise
- 1/4 cup chopped celery
- 1/4 cup chopped carrot
- 1/2 teaspoon onion powder
- 1/2 teaspoon garlic powder
- 1/4 teaspoon dill weed
- 10 slices whole wheat bread, toasted
- 5 lettuce leaves

1 In a large bowl, combine the first seven ingredients. For each sandwich, layer a slice of toast with a lettuce leaf and 1/2 cup tuna salad. Top with a second slice of toast.

cucumber sandwiches

PREP/TOTAL TIME: 15 min. | **YIELD:** 6 servings.

These bites are great for sultry summer days when something cool and refreshing is in order. Try them with sliced onions, too. KAREN SCHRIEFER, STEVENSVILLE, MARYLAND

- 1 carton (8 ounces) spreadable cream cheese
- 2 teaspoons ranch salad dressing mix
- 12 slices pumpernickel rye bread
- 2 to 3 medium cucumbers

1 In a large bowl, combine cream cheese and dressing mix. Spread on one side of each slice of bread. Peel cucumbers if desired; thinly slice and place on six slices of bread. Top with remaining bread. Serve immediately.

lemony shrimp sandwiches

PREP/TOTAL TIME: 20 min. | **YIELD:** 2 servings.

I guarantee you'll have a new favorite after you take one delicious bite of these sandwiches. The no-fuss citrus spread pairs perfectly with the shrimp.
CATHERINE FONTANA, FOX LAKE, ILLINOIS

- 1/3 cup fat-free mayonnaise
- 1 teaspoon lemon juice
- 3/4 teaspoon grated lemon peel
- 1/4 teaspoon ground coriander
- 1/8 teaspoon salt
- 1/8 teaspoon pepper
- 2 slices sourdough bread (1/2 inch thick)
- 2 Boston lettuce leaves
- 1 medium tomato, cut into 1/4-inch slices
- 6 cooked large shrimp, peeled and deveined, butterflied
- 1/2 medium ripe avocado, peeled and sliced
- 2 thin slices red onion

1 In a small bowl, combine the mayonnaise, lemon juice and peel, coriander, salt and pepper. Spread over both slices of bread. Layer each with lettuce, tomato, shrimp, avocado and onion.

sandwich for 12

PREP: 25 min. + rising | **BAKE:** 25 min. + cooling
YIELD: 12 servings.

This super sandwich always makes a big hit at church suppers and potlucks. Folks love that the onion-oat bread is homemade. MELISSA COLLIER, WICHITA FALLS, TEXAS

- 1/2 cup old-fashioned oats
- 1/2 cup boiling water
- 2 tablespoons butter
- 1 package (16 ounces) hot roll mix
- 3/4 cup warm water (110° to 115°)
- 2 eggs, lightly beaten
- 1 tablespoon dried minced onion

TOPPING:

- 1 egg
- 1 teaspoon garlic salt
- 1 tablespoon dried minced onion
- 1 tablespoon sesame seeds

FILLING:

- 1/2 cup mayonnaise
- 4 teaspoons prepared mustard
- 1/2 teaspoon prepared horseradish

Lettuce leaves

- 8 ounces thinly sliced fully cooked ham
- 8 ounces thinly sliced cooked turkey
- 1 medium green pepper, thinly sliced
- 1 medium onion, thinly sliced

- 6 ounces thinly sliced Swiss cheese
- 2 large tomatoes, thinly sliced

1 In a large bowl, combine oats, boiling water and butter; let stand for 5 minutes. Meanwhile, dissolve yeast from hot roll mix in warm water. Add to the oat mixture with eggs and onion. Add flour mixture from hot roll mix; stir well (do not knead).

2 Spread dough into a 10-in. circle on a well-greased pizza pan. Cover with plastic wrap coated with cooking spray; let rise in a warm place until doubled, about 45 minutes.

3 Beat egg and garlic salt; brush gently over dough. Sprinkle with onion and sesame seeds. Bake at 350° for 25-30 minutes or until golden brown. Remove from pan; cool on a wire rack.

4 Split lengthwise. Combine mayonnaise, mustard and horseradish; spread over cut sides of loaf. Layer with remaining filling ingredients. Cut into wedges.

chocolate peanut butter sandwiches

PREP: 5 min. + chilling | **YIELD:** 2-1/4 cups spread.

This peanut butter spread was a favorite when I was growing up. I still make it today whenever I crave a sweet, chocolaty treat. OPAL WAGONER, NORTHWOOD, OHIO

- 1/2 cup butter, cubed
- 1/2 cup honey
- 1/4 cup baking cocoa
- 1-1/3 cups creamy peanut butter
- 1/4 teaspoon vanilla extract
- 2 slices white bread, crusts removed

1 Melt butter in a small saucepan. Stir in honey and cocoa until smooth. Remove from the heat; stir in peanut butter and vanilla. Refrigerate until mixture solidifies. For each sandwich, spread 2 tablespoons between two slices of white bread.

EDITOR'S NOTE: Mixture solidifies as it cools.

beef sandwiches with beet spread

PREP/TOTAL TIME: 25 min. | **YIELD:** 8 servings.

Stack it up! This old-fashioned sensation has a zesty horseradish beet spread that will come alive in your mouth. Topped with onion, lettuce and tomato, it's one killer of a sandwich that outshines the rest. DAWN SCHUMILAS, WHITE FOX, SASKATCHEWAN

  4 ounces cream cheese, softened
  1 whole fresh beet, cooked, peeled and mashed (about 1/2 cup)
1/4 cup prepared horseradish
  2 tablespoons lemon juice
  1 tablespoon white vinegar
1-1/2 teaspoons sugar
Dash cayenne pepper
  8 hard rolls, split and toasted
  8 teaspoons butter, softened

  1 pound thinly sliced deli roast beef
  8 lettuce leaves
  8 slices tomato
  8 slices onion

1 In a small bowl, beat cream cheese and beet until blended. Beat in the horseradish, lemon juice, vinegar, sugar and cayenne.

2 Spread rolls with butter and beet spread. Layer with beef, lettuce, tomato and onion.

spinach feta croissants for 2

PREP/TOTAL TIME: 10 min. | **YIELD:** 2 servings.

I tried this meatless sandwich at a local cafe and added Italian salad dressing for a unique taste twist. You can also use mini croissants for smaller-sized servings.

DOLORES BRIGHAM, INGLEWOOD, CALIFORNIA

- 3 tablespoons Italian salad dressing
- 2 croissants, split
- 1 cup fresh baby spinach
- 1 plum tomato, thinly sliced
- 1/3 cup crumbled feta cheese

1 Brush salad dressing over the cut sides of croissants. On the bottom halves, layer with spinach, tomato and feta cheese; replace tops.

chickpea sandwich spread

PREP/TOTAL TIME: 20 min. | **YIELD:** 7 servings.

My homemade sandwich spread is a great alternative to deli lunch meat. The pickle relish gives this hummus-like mixture added zing without any extra fat.

TRISH QUINN, CHEYENNE, WYOMING

- 1/2 cup dill pickle relish
- 1/3 cup reduced-fat mayonnaise
- 1/4 cup dill pickle juice
- 1 tablespoon honey Dijon mustard
- 2 cans (15 ounces *each*) chickpeas *or* garbanzo beans, rinsed and drained
- 1/3 cup finely chopped celery
- 1/3 cup shredded carrot
- 7 whole wheat pita pocket halves
- 2 cups fresh torn spinach
- 7 tomato slices, halved

1 In a blender, combine the pickle relish, mayonnaise, pickle juice and mustard. Add one can of chickpeas; cover and process until smooth. Gradually add the remaining can of chickpeas; blend until mixture is smooth.

2 Transfer to a large bowl; stir in the celery and carrot. Line pita bread with spinach leaves and tomato slices. Place about 1/2 cup chickpea mixture in each pita half.

pumpernickel turkey hero

PREP/TOTAL TIME: 10 min. | **YIELD:** 6 servings.

You'll love the lineup of fresh sandwich ingredients stacked in between rich, dark pumpernickel. Thousand Island dressing lends flavor to each bite of this hearty creation. Slice the loaf into wedges before serving.

MILDRED SHERRER, FORT WORTH, TEXAS

- 1 round loaf (1 pound) unsliced pumpernickel bread
- 1/3 cup Thousand Island salad dressing
- 6 lettuce leaves
- 2 medium tomatoes, sliced
- 3 slices red onion, separated into rings
- 6 slices Swiss cheese
- 1 package (12 ounces) thinly sliced deli turkey

1 Cut bread in half horizontally; spread salad dressing over cut sides. On the bottom half, layer the lettuce, tomatoes, onion, half of the cheese and half of the turkey. Top with remaining cheese and turkey. Replace bread top. Slice before serving.

havarti turkey hero

PREP/TOTAL TIME: 15 min. | **YIELD:** 8 servings.

This is not your ordinary sandwich! Everyone likes the combination of chutney and chopped peanuts. I make this when I have company in the afternoon or in the evening after a night on the town. AGNES WARD, STRATFORD, ONTARIO

- 1/3 cup mango chutney
- 2 tablespoons reduced-fat mayonnaise
- 2 tablespoons chopped unsalted peanuts

Dash cayenne pepper

- 1 loaf (1 pound) French bread, halved lengthwise
- 3/4 pound thinly sliced deli turkey
- 6 lettuce leaves
- 2 ounces thinly sliced Havarti cheese
- 1 medium Red Delicious apple, cored and cut into thin rings

1 In a small bowl, combine the chutney, mayonnaise, peanuts and cayenne; spread evenly over the cut side of bread bottom. Layer with turkey, lettuce, cheese and apple. Replace bread top. Cut into eight slices.

chicken salad sandwiches

PREP/TOTAL TIME: 15 min. | **YIELD:** 8 servings.

I made these simple yet special delights for a birthday party. Tangy cranberries and crunchy celery liven up the sandwich filling. Leftover turkey works well in place of the chicken, too. SHANNON TUCKER, LAND O' LAKES, FLORIDA

- 1/2 cup mayonnaise
- 2 tablespoons honey Dijon mustard
- 1/4 teaspoon pepper
- 2 cups cubed rotisserie chicken
- 1 cup (4 ounces) shredded Swiss cheese
- 1/2 cup chopped celery
- 1/2 cup dried cranberries
- 1/4 cup chopped walnuts
- 1/2 teaspoon dried parsley flakes
- 8 lettuce leaves
- 16 slices pumpernickel bread

1 In a large bowl, combine the mayonnaise, mustard and pepper. Stir in the chicken, cheese, celery, cranberries, walnuts and parsley.

2 Place lettuce on eight slices of bread; top each with 1/2 cup chicken salad and remaining bread.

fresh mozzarella sandwiches

PREP/TOTAL TIME: 15 min. | **YIELD:** 4 servings.

This fast, fresh sandwich is ideal for alfresco dining, especially when it's too warm to turn on the oven. I like to pair it with a fruity white wine and pasta salad or potato chips. I sometimes add avocado and Walla Walla onions to make use of my homegrown ingredients.

STACEY JOHNSON, TACOMA, WASHINGTON

- 8 slices sourdough bread, toasted
- 1/4 cup wasabi mayonnaise
- 1/2 pound fresh mozzarella cheese, sliced
- 2 medium tomatoes, sliced
- 4 thin slices sweet onion
- 8 fresh basil leaves

1 Spread toast with mayonnaise. On four slices, layer with cheese, tomatoes, onion and basil; top with remaining toast.

tip Compared to the more firm texture of most commercially produced mozzarella, fresh mozzarella is soft and moist. The flavor is mild, delicate and somewhat milky. Fresh mozzarella is usually shaped into balls and stored in brine. After buying fresh mozzarella, it should be refrigerated in the brine and eaten within a few days.

super-duper tuna sandwiches

PREP/TOTAL TIME: 15 min. | **YIELD:** 4 servings.

If packing this fantastic sandwich for a brown-bag lunch, keep the bread separate from the salad so it doesn't get soggy. You can also try serving the tuna salad with crackers, as a wrap or on lettuce.

RENEE BARTOLOMEO, INDIANOLA, IOWA

- 2 cans (5 ounces *each*) light water-packed tuna, drained and flaked
- 1/3 cup shredded peeled apple
- 1/3 cup finely shredded cabbage
- 1/3 cup finely shredded carrot
- 3 tablespoons finely chopped celery
- 3 tablespoons finely chopped onion
- 3 tablespoons sweet pickle relish
- 2 tablespoons reduced-fat mayonnaise
- 8 slices whole wheat bread

1 In a large bowl, combine the first eight ingredients. Spread 1/2 cup tuna mixture over four slices of bread; top with remaining bread slices.

bistro turkey sandwiches

PREP/TOTAL TIME: 30 min. | **YIELD:** 6 servings.

Sweet and savory flavors combine in this quick, healthful sandwich. The apples give an unexpected crunch. You can substitute them with pears for a tasty change of pace.

VERONICA CALLAGHAN, GLASTONBURY, CONNECTICUT

1	small red onion, thinly sliced
4	teaspoons brown sugar, *divided*
1	tablespoon olive oil
1/4	teaspoon salt
1/8	teaspoon cayenne pepper
1/4	cup Dijon mustard
1	tablespoon apple cider *or* unsweetened apple juice
6	wheat sandwich buns, split
6	Bibb *or* Boston lettuce leaves
1	medium pear, peeled and thinly sliced
1	pound cooked turkey breast, thinly sliced
1/4	cup loosely packed basil leaves
6	tablespoons crumbled Gorgonzola cheese

1 In a small skillet over medium heat, cook onion and 1 teaspoon brown sugar in oil for 8-10 minutes or until golden brown, stirring frequently. Stir in salt and cayenne.

2 Combine the mustard, apple cider and remaining brown sugar; spread over bun bottoms. Layer with lettuce, pear, turkey, basil and cheese. Top with caramelized onion. Replace tops.

ham and swiss bagels

PREP/TOTAL TIME: 10 min. | **YIELD:** 2 servings.

You can whip up this super easy sandwich in about 10 minutes. Pineapple and cream cheese give it a fun twist.

BEV BRONLEEWE, LORRAINE, KANSAS

1/4	cup whipped cream cheese
2	tablespoons honey mustard
2	whole wheat bagels, split
1	slice Swiss cheese, halved
2	slices canned pineapple
8	thin slices deli smoked ham
2	lettuce leaves

1 In a small bowl, combine cream cheese and mustard until smooth; spread over the cut sides of bagels. On bagel bottoms, layer with cheese, pineapple, ham and lettuce. Replace bagel tops.

tip Here's a super way to use up leftover bagels. Cut them into very thin slices, layer in a baking pan, spritz with nonstick cooking spray and sprinkle with different seasonings. Try garlic powder or dried basil on egg or onion bagels, and cinnamon and sugar on raisin bagels. Place the pan in a 350° oven for about 15-20 minutes or until the bagel slices are crispy. They're delicious and great with dips. Plus, they're less expensive than bagel chips at the store.

apple-swiss turkey sandwiches

PREP/TOTAL TIME: 15 min. | **YIELD:** 4 servings.

Honey mustard adds a sweet tang to this hearty concoction layered between slices of nutritious multi-grain bread. These delicious sandwiches pack well to take to the office or on the trail. GLORIA UPDYKE, FRONT ROYAL, VIRGINIA

3 tablespoons honey mustard

8 slices multi-grain bread, toasted

2 medium apples, thinly sliced

8 slices reduced-fat Swiss cheese

1/2 cup thinly sliced cucumber

8 ounces thinly sliced cooked turkey breast

1 Lightly spread mustard on each slice of toast; set aside. Place apples on a microwave-safe plate and microwave, uncovered, on high for 1 minute or until slightly softened.

2 Arrange half of the apple slices and cheese on 4 slices of toast. Top with cucumber and turkey. Add remaining apple and cheese slices. Top with remaining toast, mustard side down.

EDITOR'S NOTE: This recipe was tested in a 1,100-watt microwave.

creamy beef sandwiches

PREP/TOTAL TIME: 20 min. | **YIELD:** 6 servings.

This is a quick way to create a sandwich with a special taste. The creamy dressing and combination of beef and cheese make them ideal for lunches on the go.

DORIS BYERLY, MONDOVI, WISCONSIN

- 1/2 cup mayonnaise
- 2 to 3 tablespoons prepared ranch salad dressing
- 2 packages (2-1/2 ounces *each*) thinly sliced dried beef, chopped
- 1 cup (4 ounces) shredded cheddar cheese
- 12 slices white bread
- 1-1/2 cups shredded lettuce

1 In a small bowl, combine mayonnaise and ranch dressing. Stir in the beef and cheese. Spread about 1/3 cup on six slices of bread; top with lettuce and remaining bread.

blts with raisin-avocado spread

PREP/TOTAL TIME: 20 min. | **YIELD:** 6 servings.

Tired of the same old BLT? Forgo the mayonnaise and try my blend of cream cheese, avocado and raisins to dress up the traditional favorite.

VERONICA CALLAGHAN, GLASTONBURY, CONNECTICUT

- 1 medium ripe avocado, peeled and cubed
- 4 ounces cream cheese, cubed
- 1/2 cup golden raisins
- 1/4 cup pine nuts
- 1/4 cup minced fresh parsley
- 1/2 teaspoon salt
- 1/4 teaspoon pepper
- 12 slices sourdough bread, toasted
- 12 bacon strips, cooked and halved
- 12 romaine leaves
- 6 slices tomato

1 In a food processor, combine the first seven ingredients; cover and process until blended. Spread evenly over six slices of toast. Layer with bacon, lettuce and tomato. Top with remaining toast.

tip To easily remove the pit from an avocado, wash the avocado and cut in half lengthwise, cutting around the seed. Twist halves in opposite directions to separate. Slip a tablespoon under the seed to loosen it from the fruit. To remove avocado flesh from the skin, loosen it from the skin with a large spoon and scoop out. Slice the peeled avocado as desired. Or cut into unpeeled wedges and slice between the flesh and the skin.

blue cheese clubs

PREP/TOTAL TIME: 25 min. | **YIELD:** 4 servings.

These triple-deckers are piled high with fresh ingredients and get an tantalizing flavor from a zippy blue cheese spread. You'll be surprised how easy they are to make.
NANCY JO LEFFLER, DEPAUW, INDIANA

- 1 package (3 ounces) cream cheese, softened
- 1/2 cup crumbled blue cheese
- 4 tablespoons mayonnaise, *divided*
- 1 teaspoon dried minced onion

Dash salt and pepper

Dash Worcestershire sauce

- 8 slices white bread, toasted
- 8 slices tomato
- 8 slices deli turkey
- 4 slices Swiss cheese
- 4 slices whole wheat bread, toasted
- 8 bacon strips, cooked
- 4 lettuce leaves

1 In a small bowl, beat cream cheese until smooth. Beat in the blue cheese, 1 tablespoon mayonnaise, onion, salt, pepper and Worcestershire sauce until blended.

2 Spread over four slices of white bread; layer with tomato, turkey, Swiss cheese, wheat bread, bacon and lettuce. Spread remaining mayonnaise over remaining white bread; place over lettuce. Secure with toothpicks; cut into triangles.

cashew turkey salad sandwiches

PREP/TOTAL TIME: 15 min. | **YIELD:** 4 servings.

One bite and you'll be hooked on this sweet and savory sandwich. Turkey and cashews give it a double punch of protein to help keep you full. MARY WILHELM, SPARTA, WISCONSIN

- 1-1/2 cups cubed cooked turkey breast
- 1/4 cup thinly sliced celery
- 2 tablespoons chopped dried apricots
- 2 tablespoons chopped unsalted cashews
- 1 green onion, chopped
- 1/4 cup reduced-fat mayonnaise
- 2 tablespoons reduced-fat plain yogurt
- 1/4 teaspoon salt
- 1/4 teaspoon pepper
- 4 lettuce leaves
- 8 slices pumpernickel bread

1 In a small bowl, combine the turkey, celery, apricots, cashews and onion. Combine the mayonnaise, yogurt, salt and pepper; add to turkey mixture and stir to coat.

2 Place a lettuce leaf on half of the bread slices; top each with 1/2 cup turkey salad and remaining bread.

lime-cilantro turkey hoagies

PREP/TOTAL TIME: 10 min. | **YIELD:** 2 servings.

Infuse a burst of flavor to an ordinary turkey and cheese sandwich with mayo spiked with lime juice and cilantro.

TASTE OF HOME TEST KITCHEN

1/4	cup mayonnaise
1-1/4	teaspoons minced fresh cilantro
1/4	teaspoon lime juice
1/8	teaspoon sugar
1/8	teaspoon white vinegar
2	hoagie buns, split
6	slices (3/4 ounce *each*) deli turkey
2	slices (1 ounce *each*) provolone cheese
4	slices tomato
2	lettuce leaves

1 In a bowl, whisk the mayonnaise, cilantro, lime juice, sugar and vinegar. Evenly spread over cut side of buns. On bun bottoms, layer with turkey, provolone, tomato and lettuce; replace bun tops.

tip With its slightly sharp flavor, cilantro—also known as Chinese parsley—gives a distinctive taste to many dishes. (The spice coriander comes from the seed of the cilantro plant.) Like all other fresh herbs, cilantro should be used as soon as possible. For short-term storage, immerse the freshly cut stems in water about 2 inches deep. Cover leaves loosely with a plastic bag and refrigerate for several days. Wash just before using.

mom's egg salad sandwiches

PREP/TOTAL TIME: 15 min. | **YIELD:** 6 servings.

I'm proud to share this old-fashioned favorite from my mother's recipe files. Green pepper and celery add crunch to the classic sandwich filling, while cream cheese makes it extra rich. It's also delicious tucked inside pita pockets.

TIRZAH LUJAN, WICHITA FALLS, TEXAS

1	package (3 ounces) cream cheese, softened
1/4	cup mayonnaise
1	tablespoon chili sauce
1/2	teaspoon salt
1/8	teaspoon pepper
8	hard-cooked eggs, chopped
1/4	cup chopped green pepper
1/4	cup chopped celery
2	tablespoons finely chopped onion
2	tablespoons diced pimientos, drained
1	tablespoon minced fresh parsley
12	slices white bread
6	lettuce leaves
6	slices tomato

1 In a small bowl, beat the cream cheese, mayonnaise, chili sauce, salt and pepper. Stir in the eggs, green pepper, celery, onion, pimientos and parsley.

2 On six slices of bread, layer lettuce, tomato and 1/2 cup egg salad. Top with remaining bread.

cherry-chicken salad croissants

PREP/TOTAL TIME: 15 min. | **YIELD:** 7 servings.

I love cherries, so I decided to combine them with chicken salad tucked inside a buttery croissant. My family was pleased with the delicious result!

MARTHA GOODRICH, WILMINGTON, DELAWARE

2-1/2 cups cubed cooked chicken breast
2/3 cup dried cherries
1/3 cup chopped celery
1/3 cup chopped tart apple
1/3 cup chopped pecans, toasted
1/2 cup mayonnaise
4 teaspoons buttermilk
1/2 teaspoon salt
1/8 teaspoon pepper
7 croissants, split

1 In a large bowl, combine the chicken, cherries, celery, apple and pecans. In another bowl, combine the mayonnaise, buttermilk, salt and pepper; add to chicken mixture and mix well. Spoon 1/2 cup chicken salad onto each croissant.

brickyard bistro sandwich

PREP/TOTAL TIME: 15 min. | **YIELD:** 4 servings.

This is my go-to sandwich for tailgaits and game-day parties. It features three kinds of meat, so even the heartiest of appetites will be satisfied. TASTE OF HOME TEST KITCHEN

1 loaf (1 pound) focaccia bread
2 tablespoons olive oil
1 tablespoon balsamic vinegar
2 teaspoons minced fresh oregano
1 teaspoon minced fresh rosemary
2 slices red onion, separated into rings
2 ounces sliced deli smoked turkey
2 ounces thinly sliced hard salami
2 ounces sliced deli roast beef
2 ounces sliced provolone cheese
1 plum tomato, sliced
2 lettuce leaves

1 Cut focaccia in half horizontally. In a small bowl, combine the oil, vinegar, oregano and rosemary; brush over cut sides of bread.

2 On bread bottom, layer with the onion, turkey, salami, roast beef, cheese, tomato and lettuce; replace bread top. Cut into four wedges.

savory sandwich ring

PREP: 20 min. | **BAKE:** 25 min. + cooling | **YIELD:** 8-10 servings.

I first made this alternative to a submarine sandwich for a potluck. Now it's a mainstay on my menu for gatherings or when my family is tired of ordinary meat-and-cheese sandwiches. SUSANNE EBERSOL, BIRD-IN-HAND, PENNSYLVANIA

- 2 tubes (11 ounces *each*) crusty French bread dough
- 2 teaspoons olive oil
- 3 garlic cloves, pressed
- 1/2 teaspoon Italian seasoning
- 1/3 cup Italian salad dressing
- 1/2 pound thinly sliced deli ham
- 1/4 pound sliced process American *or* Swiss cheese, halved
- 1/4 to 1/2 pound thinly sliced deli roast beef *or* turkey
- 2 cups shredded lettuce
- 1 medium red onion, thinly sliced
- 1 medium green pepper, thinly sliced
- 1 medium tomato, thinly sliced

1 Place both loaves of dough seam side down on a greased 14-in. pizza pan, forming one large ring; pinch ends to seal. With a sharp knife, make eight 1/2-in.-deep slashes across the top of dough; lightly brush with oil.

2 Spread garlic over oil; sprinkle with Italian seasoning. Bake at 350° for 25-30 minutes or until golden brown. Cool for 10 minutes before removing from pan to a wire rack to cool completely.

3 To assemble, cut the bread in half horizontally. Brush salad dressing over cut sides. Layer the bottom half with ham, cheese, beef, lettuce, onion, green pepper and tomato; replace top. Serve immediately. Refrigerate leftovers.

country ham sandwiches

PREP/TOTAL TIME: 5 min. | **YIELD:** 2 servings.

Smoked cheddar and a creamy garlic-infused spread lend an irresistible appeal to the classic ham sandwich. Try it alongside a steaming bowl of soup on a cool, rainy day.
JENNIFER PARHAM, BROWNS SUMMIT, NORTH CAROLINA

- 2 tablespoons mayonnaise
- 2 tablespoons sour cream
- 1/8 teaspoon garlic powder
- 4 slices whole wheat bread
- 2 ounces smoked cheddar cheese, sliced
- 4 slices tomato
- 4 ounces thinly sliced deli ham
- 2 lettuce leaves

1 In a small bowl, combine the mayonnaise, sour cream and garlic powder. Spread over two slices of bread. Layer each with cheese, tomato, ham and lettuce. Top with remaining bread.

tip Savory Sandwich Ring is perfect for outdoor get-togethers such as tailgaits, beach parties and picnics. Simply pack a bag of chips, some deli pasta salad and brownies from the bakery for a no-fuss menu. Don't forget a serrated knife to slice the sandwich!

turkey salad sandwiches

PREP/TOTAL TIME: 15 min. | **YIELD:** 6 servings.

Inspired by a delicious turkey salad sandwich at a local deli, I developed my own version to suit my family's tastes. Serve this on croissants for an elegant luncheon or on hearty whole-grain bread for a filling meal. Use precooked bacon and leftover turkey to keep prep easy.

MERRIJANE RICE, BOUNTIFUL, UTAH

10	ounces deli turkey, cubed
2	cups torn romaine
6	bacon strips, cooked and crumbled
1/2	cup shredded Swiss cheese
1/2	cup mayonnaise
1/3	cup frozen peas, thawed
2	green onions, thinly sliced
1/4	teaspoon pepper
12	slices whole wheat bread

1 In a large bowl, combine the first eight ingredients. Spoon 2/3 cup mixture on each of six bread slices. Top with remaining bread slices.

artichoke-lamb sandwich loaves

PREP: 50 min. + marinating | **BAKE:** 1 hour 20 min. + chilling
YIELD: 24 servings.

These tender sandwiches will surely become the talk of any get-together. I hollow out sourdough baguettes before filling them with cucumber, cheese and marinated lamb and artichokes. Simply delicious, the mouthwatering bites are perfect for a spring brunch.

HELEN HASSLER, DENVER, PENNSYLVANIA

1/2	cup lemon juice
1/2	cup olive oil
6	garlic cloves, minced
2	tablespoons minced fresh rosemary
1	teaspoon salt
1/4	teaspoon cayenne pepper
1	boneless leg of lamb (2-1/2 pounds)
2	cans (14 ounces *each*) water-packed artichoke hearts, rinsed and drained
2/3	cup plus 6 tablespoons reduced-fat balsamic vinaigrette, *divided*
2	sourdough baguettes (1 pound *each*)
1	medium cucumber, thinly sliced
2	medium tomatoes, thinly sliced
1	package (5.3 ounces) fresh goat cheese, sliced

1 In a large resealable plastic bag, combine the first six ingredients; add lamb. Seal bag and turn to coat. Refrigerate for 8 hours or overnight.

2 Drain and discard marinade. Place lamb on a rack in a shallow roasting pan. Bake, uncovered, at 325° for 80-90 minutes or until meat reaches desired doneness (for medium-rare, a meat thermometer should read 145°; medium, 160°; well-done, 170°). Cool to room temperature. Cover and refrigerate for at least 2 hours.

3 Place artichokes in a resealable plastic bag; add 2/3 cup vinaigrette. Seal bag and turn to coat; let stand for 10 minutes. Drain and discard marinade.

4 Cut lamb into thin slices. Cut each baguette in half horizontally. Carefully hollow out top and bottom, leaving a 3/4-in. shell. Brush the bottom half of each loaf with 2 tablespoons vinaigrette. Layer with cucumber, tomatoes, lamb and artichokes; drizzle with remaining vinaigrette. Top with goat cheese.

5 Replace bread tops and press down firmly; wrap tightly in plastic wrap. Refrigerate for at least 2 hours. Cut into slices.

hearty veggie sandwiches

PREP/TOTAL TIME: 15 min. | **YIELD:** 2 servings.

My sister and I created this one day when we had some bagels left over from breakfast. We have a penchant for everything bagels (bagels with roasted seeds on top), but you can use any variety of your choice. CAROLINE MUNOZ, AUSTIN, MINNESOTA

2 tablespoons mayonnaise
2 teaspoons Dijon mustard
2 bagels, split
2 lettuce leaves
1 medium ripe avocado, peeled and sliced
2 large slices tomato

1 slice sweet onion, separated into rings
Salt and pepper to taste

1 In a small bowl, combine mayonnaise and mustard; spread over cut sides of bagels. On bagel bottoms, layer the lettuce, avocado, tomato and onion. Sprinkle with salt and pepper. Replace bagel tops.

BURRITOS MADE EASY, PG. 65

wraps & roll-ups

CHICKEN LETTUCE WRAPS, PG. 71

VEGETARIAN HUMMUS WRAPS, PG. 74

pepperoni stromboli

PREP: 25 min. + rising | **BAKE:** 30 min. | **YIELD:** about 16 servings.

I've made this comforting stromboli many times. It's perfect for tailgates and game-day parties. Made with convenient frozen bread dough, the sandwiches always satisfy huge appetites. SHELLEY BANZHAF, MAYWOOD, NEBRASKA

- 2 loaves (1 pound *each*) frozen bread dough, thawed
- 2 eggs, lightly beaten
- 1/3 cup olive oil
- 1/2 teaspoon *each* garlic powder, salt and pepper
- 1/2 teaspoon ground mustard
- 1/2 teaspoon dried oregano
- 1 pound lean ground beef (90% lean), cooked and drained
- 1 package (3-1/2 ounces) sliced pepperoni
- 2 cups (8 ounces) shredded part-skim mozzarella cheese
- 1 cup (4 ounces) shredded cheddar cheese
- 1 small onion, chopped

1 Place each loaf of bread dough in a greased large bowl, turning once to grease top. Cover and let rise in a warm place until doubled, about 45 minutes. Punch down. Roll each loaf into a 15-in. x 12-in. rectangle.

2 In a small bowl, combine the eggs, oil and seasonings. Brush over dough to within 1/2 in. of edges; set remaining egg mixture aside. Layer with beef, pepperoni, cheeses and onion on dough to within 1/2 in. of edges. Roll up, jelly-roll style, beginning with a long side. Seal the edges well.

3 Place seam side down on greased baking sheets. Brush with remaining egg mixture. Bake at 375° for 30-35 minutes or until lightly browned. Let stand for 5-10 minutes before cutting.

asian meatless wraps

PREP/TOTAL TIME: 10 min. | **YIELD:** 4 servings.

I purchased a package of vegetarian chicken patties but needed a creative way to serve them. This recipe, an impromptu creation on a busy weeknight, turned out so well—my husband never knew it wasn't "real" chicken! HEIDI HEIMGARTNER, BLOOMING PRAIRIE, MINNESOTA

- 4 frozen vegetarian chicken patties
- 1 cup coleslaw mix
- 1/3 cup Asian toasted sesame salad dressing
- 4 flour tortillas (10 inches), warmed
- 1/2 cup chow mein noodles
- 1/4 cup sliced almonds

1 Microwave patties according to package directions. Meanwhile, combine coleslaw mix and dressing; set aside.

2 Cut the patties in half; place two halves off center on each tortilla; top with 3 tablespoon coleslaw mixture, 2 tablespoons chow mein noodles and 1 tablespoon almonds. Fold sides and ends over filling and roll up.

EDITOR'S NOTE: This recipe was tested in a 1,100-watt microwave.

tip Feel free to use traditional chicken patties in these Asian wraps if you prefer. You can purchase frozen store-bought patties or make your own using 1 pound ground chicken mixed with a few chopped scallions, freshly grated ginger and a finely chopped clove of garlic.

zippy blt wraps

PREP/TOTAL TIME: 15 min. | **YIELD:** 4 servings.

I love BLT sandwiches and whole wheat wraps, so I came up with this recipe to enjoy the best of both worlds. Salsa, avocado and garlic powder give them a unique taste twist.

TRISHA THIELEN, ABERDEEN, SOUTH DAKOTA

- 3 tablespoons mayonnaise
- 4 teaspoons salsa
- 4 whole wheat tortillas (8 inches), room temperature
- 1/4 teaspoon garlic powder

Dash *each* salt and pepper

- 12 slices ready-to-serve fully cooked bacon
- 4 lettuce leaves
- 1 large tomato, sliced
- 1/2 medium ripe avocado, peeled and sliced

1 Spread mayonnaise and salsa down the center of each tortilla. Sprinkle with the garlic powder, salt and pepper. Layer with bacon strips, lettuce, tomato and avocado; roll up tightly.

tuscan steak flatbreads

PREP: 25 min. | **GRILL:** 15 min. | **YIELD:** 4 servings.

Take flatbreads grilled in pesto, wrap them around steak, top with cheese and you have an instant hit! Guests will love the fun presentation and mouthwatering flavor.

MICHAEL COHEN, LOS ANGELES, CALIFORNIA

SUN-DRIED TOMATO PESTO:
- 1/3 cup packed fresh parsley sprigs
- 2 tablespoons fresh basil leaves
- 1 garlic clove, quartered
- 2 tablespoons grated Parmesan cheese

- 2 tablespoons oil-packed sun-dried tomatoes, patted dry
- 2 tablespoons sherry
- 1/4 teaspoon salt

Dash pepper
- 1/4 cup olive oil

STEAK FLATBREADS:
- 1 beef top sirloin steak (3/4 inch thick and 1-1/4 pounds)
- 1/4 teaspoon salt
- 1/4 teaspoon pepper
- 4 flatbreads *or* whole pita breads
- 2 tablespoons olive oil
- 1 cup (4 ounces) shredded fontina cheese
- 1/4 cup fresh basil leaves, thinly sliced

1 For pesto, place the parsley, basil and garlic in a food processor; cover and pulse until chopped. Add the Parmesan cheese, tomatoes, sherry, salt and pepper; cover and process until blended. While processing, gradually add oil in a steady stream. Set aside.

2 Sprinkle steak with salt and pepper. Grill, covered, over medium heat for 6-10 minutes on each side or until meat reaches desired doneness (for medium-rare, a meat thermometer should read 145°; medium, 160°; well-done, 170°). Remove and keep warm.

3 Brush one side of each flatbread with oil; place oiled side down on grill rack. Grill, covered, over medium heat for 1-2 minutes or until heated through.

4 Spread pesto over grilled side of flatbreads. Cut steak into thin strips; place over pesto. Top with fontina cheese and basil.

grandma's french tuna salad wraps

PREP/TOTAL TIME: 15 min. | **YIELD:** 2 servings.

My French Canadian grandmother always added chopped egg to her tuna salad. I made my own version by tossing in some veggies for complete nutrition and turning it into a wrap. It's fun, and we enjoy our grandma's memory with each bite. JENNIFER MAGREY, STERLING, CONNECTICUT

- 1 can (5 ounces) light water-packed tuna, drained and flaked
- 1 celery rib, finely chopped
- 1/4 cup fat-free mayonnaise
- 1/4 teaspoon pepper
- 2 whole wheat tortillas (8 inches), room temperature
- 1/2 cup shredded lettuce
- 1 small carrot, shredded
- 4 slices tomato
- 2 slices red onion, separated into rings
- 1 hard-cooked egg, sliced

1 In a small bowl, combine the tuna, celery, mayonnaise and pepper. Spoon tuna mixture down the center of each tortilla. Top with lettuce, carrot, tomato, onion and egg. Roll up tightly; secure with toothpicks.

tip Jazz up tuna salad by adding shredded cheddar cheese to the mix. It thickens the mixture so it doesn't squeeze out of the sandwich or wrap.

buffalo chicken roll-ups

PREP/TOTAL TIME: 30 min. | **YIELD:** 8 servings.

Featuring tender chicken, crunchy vegetables and a spicy buffalo wing sauce, this fuss-free meal quickly became a favorite in our house. Feel free to change the veggies to suit your tastes. SARAH GOTTSCHALK, RICHMOND, INDIANA

- 1-1/2 pounds chicken tenderloins
- 1 cup buffalo wing sauce, *divided*
- 8 lettuce leaves
- 8 flour tortillas (10 inches), warmed
- 16 bacon strips, cooked
- 1 small green pepper, cut into strips
- 1/2 cup ranch salad dressing

1 In a large skillet, bring chicken and 1/2 cup buffalo wing sauce to a boil. Reduce heat; cover and simmer for 10-12 minutes or until meat is no longer pink. Remove from the heat; cool slightly. Shred chicken with two forks.

2 Place a lettuce leaf on each tortilla; spoon about 1/2 cup chicken mixture down the center. Top with bacon and green pepper. Drizzle with ranch dressing and remaining buffalo wing sauce; roll up.

chili chicken enchiladas

PREP: 20 min. | **BAKE:** 20 min. | **YIELD:** 2 servings.

These hearty Southwestern enchiladas turn an ordinary meal into a fiesta! DOROTHY PRITCHETT, WILLS POINT, TEXAS

- 1 medium onion, thinly sliced
- 1 tablespoon butter
- 1 package (3 ounces) cream cheese, cubed
- 2 tablespoons canned chopped green chilies
- 1/8 teaspoon salt
- 4 flour tortillas (8 inches)
- 2 tablespoons canola oil
- 3/4 cup shredded cooked chicken
- 1 tablespoon 2% milk
- 1 cup (4 ounces) shredded Monterey Jack cheese

Chopped green onions and sliced ripe olives, optional

1 In a small skillet, saute onion in butter until tender. Remove from the heat. Stir in the cream cheese, chilies and salt until blended.

2 In another skillet, cook tortillas in oil over medium heat until warmed and lightly browned on both sides. Drain on paper towels. Spoon a fourth of cream cheese mixture down center of each tortilla. Sprinkle with chicken. Roll up and place seam side down in an 8-in. square baking dish coated with cooking spray.

3 Bake, uncovered, at 350° for 15 minutes. Brush tops with milk; sprinkle with cheese. Bake 5-10 minutes longer or until cheese is melted. Sprinkle with green onions and olives if desired.

asian chicken salad

PREP/TOTAL TIME: 20 min. | **YIELD:** 8 servings.

I serve this salad in lettuce leaves or in pita pockets to friends who enjoy something a bit out of the ordinary. This is fast, easy, a bit exotic and, best of all, delicious. If you like peanut butter, this is the chicken salad for you! MARY BERGFELD, EUGENE, OREGON

- 3/4 cup reduced-fat sesame ginger salad dressing
- 1/2 cup creamy peanut butter
- 1 tablespoon sesame oil
- 2 to 3 teaspoons cider vinegar
- 1 teaspoon salt
- 1/2 teaspoon crushed red pepper flakes
- 1/4 teaspoon pepper
- 3 packages (6 ounces *each*) ready-to-use grilled chicken breast strips
- 4 cups chopped cucumbers
- 1 cup chopped sweet red pepper
- 3/4 cup chopped green onions
- 1/4 cup grated carrot
- 8 Bibb *or* Boston lettuce leaves

Chopped fresh cilantro, optional

1 In a small bowl, whisk the first seven ingredients. In a large bowl, combine the chicken, cucumbers, pepper, onions and carrot. Drizzle with dressing; toss to coat. Chill until serving. Serve on lettuce leaves. Garnish with cilantro if desired.

tip When a recipe calls for green onions, keep things easy and fast by cutting them with a kitchen scissors rather than a knife. If the recipe calls for quite a few, grab a bunch at one time and snip away. You're done before you know it, and this method will save you from having to wash a cutting board.

lime jalapeno turkey wraps

PREP/TOTAL TIME: 15 min. | **YIELD:** 2 servings.

When I was growing up, my grandfather often treated me to his famous Southwestern-style wraps. I make them for my own family now, although I've tweaked his original recipe a little to suit our tastes. MARY JO AMOS, NOEL, MISSOURI

- 3 lettuce leaves
- 1 cup shredded cooked turkey breast (6 ounces)
- 2 tablespoons chopped seeded tomato
- 1 green onion, thinly sliced
- 1 teaspoon lime juice
- 1-1/2 teaspoons finely chopped jalapeno pepper
- 1/8 teaspoon sugar
- 1/8 teaspoon salt
- 1/8 teaspoon garlic powder
- 1/8 teaspoon pepper
- 2 flour tortillas (8 inches), room temperature
- 2 red onion rings (1/4 to 1/2 inch thick)
- 2 pitted ripe *or* pimiento-stuffed olives, optional

1 Chop one lettuce leaf; set aside the remaining leaves. In a small bowl, combine the turkey, chopped lettuce, tomato, green onion, lime juice, jalapeno, sugar, salt, garlic powder and pepper; set the mixture aside.

2 Place one lettuce leaf on each tortilla. Spoon half the filling off center on each. Fold one end over filling and roll up. Slide each wrap through the middle of an onion ring. Secure roll-up with a toothpick near the onion ring; top each with an olive if desired.

EDITOR'S NOTE: Wear disposable gloves when cutting hot peppers; the oils can burn skin. Avoid touching your face.

burritos made easy

PREP/TOTAL TIME: 30 min. | **YIELD:** 8 burritos.

These hearty burritos are packed with a zesty bean and beef filling. The recipe makes eight big servings and they're easy to transport, so they're great for potlucks or anytime you need to feed a crowd. JENNIFER MCKINNEY, WASHINGTON, ILLINOIS

- 1 pound lean ground beef (90% lean)
- 1/4 cup chopped onion
- 1 can (15 ounces) chili with beans
- 1-1/4 cups chunky salsa
- 1/4 cup chopped green chilies
- 8 flour tortillas (8 inches), warmed
- 8 slices process American cheese

Taco sauce and shredded lettuce, optional

1 In a large skillet, cook beef and onion over medium heat until meat is no longer pink; drain. Stir in the chili, salsa and chilies. Bring to a boil. Reduce heat; simmer, uncovered, for 5 minutes.

2 Spoon about 1/2 cupful beef mixture off center on each tortilla. Top each with a slice of cheese; roll up. Serve with taco sauce and lettuce if desired.

chicken satay wraps

PREP/TOTAL TIME: 15 min. | **YIELD:** 4 servings.

Why go out for Thai food when you can make it at home? Feel free to use rotisserie chicken or refrigerated grilled chicken strips to speed up preparation.

TASTE OF HOME TEST KITCHEN

- 2 tablespoons olive oil
- 2 tablespoons creamy peanut butter
- 2 green onions, chopped
- 1 teaspoon reduced-sodium soy sauce
- 1/4 teaspoon pepper
- 2 cups sliced cooked chicken
- 1 cup coleslaw mix
- 4 flour tortillas (8 inches), room temperature

1 In a large bowl, whisk the oil, peanut butter, onions, soy sauce and pepper until combined. Add the chicken and toss to coat. Sprinkle 1/4 cup coleslaw mix over each tortilla; top with chicken mixture. Roll up tightly.

super flatbread roll-ups

PREP: 40 min. + rising | **GRILL:** 15 min. | **YIELD:** 4 servings.

My kids love wraps, but this Mediterranean version is their favorite. I altered the original recipe by using whole wheat flour and cutting back on the salt. FAY STRAIT, WAUKEE, IOWA

- 1/2 teaspoon active dry yeast
- 1/2 cup warm water (110° to 115°)
- 1 teaspoon olive oil
- 1/2 teaspoon salt

- 1/3 cup whole wheat flour
- 1 cup all-purpose flour

FILLING:

- 1 beef flank steak (1 pound)
- 1/2 teaspoon salt
- 1/4 teaspoon pepper
- 1 cup shredded lettuce
- 1/4 cup sliced ripe olives
- 2 tablespoons crumbled feta cheese

1 In a small bowl, dissolve yeast in warm water. Add the oil, salt, whole wheat flour and 3/4 cup all-purpose flour; beat on medium speed for 3 minutes. Stir in enough remaining flour to form a firm dough.

2 Turn onto a lightly floured surface; knead until smooth and elastic, about 6-8 minutes. Place in a large bowl coated with cooking spray, turning once to coat the top. Cover and let rise in a warm place until doubled, about 45 minutes.

3 Punch dough down. Turn onto a lightly floured surface; divide into four portions. Roll each into an 8-in. circle.

4 Heat a large nonstick skillet coated with cooking spray over medium heat; add a portion of dough. Cook for 30-60 seconds or until bubbles form on top. Turn and cook until the second side is golden brown. Remove and keep warm. Repeat with remaining dough, adding cooking spray as needed.

5 Moisten a paper towel with cooking oil; using long-handled tongs, lightly coat the grill rack. Sprinkle steak with salt and pepper. Grill, covered, over medium-high heat or broil 4 in. from the heat for 6-8 minutes on each side or until meat reaches desired doneness (for medium-rare, a meat thermometer should read 145°; medium, 160°; well-done, 170°).

6 Let stand for 5 minutes before cutting steak thinly across the grain. Serve on warm flatbreads with lettuce, olives and cheese.

spinach 'n' broccoli enchiladas

PREP: 25 min. | **BAKE:** 25 min. | **YIELD:** 8 servings.

I top this satisfying meatless meal with shredded lettuce and serve it with extra picante sauce. It's quick, easy, filled with fresh flavor and good for you, too! LESLEY TRAGESSER, CHARLESTON, MISSOURI

- 1 medium onion, chopped
- 2 teaspoons olive oil
- 1 package (10 ounces) frozen chopped spinach, thawed and squeezed dry
- 1 cup finely chopped fresh broccoli
- 1 cup picante sauce, *divided*
- 1/2 teaspoon garlic powder
- 1/2 teaspoon ground cumin
- 1 cup (8 ounces) 1% cottage cheese
- 1 cup (4 ounces) shredded reduced-fat cheddar cheese, *divided*
- 8 flour tortillas (8 inches), warmed

1 In a large nonstick skillet over medium heat, cook and stir onion in oil until tender. Add the spinach, broccoli, 1/3 cup picante sauce, garlic powder and cumin; heat through.

2 Remove from the heat; stir in the cottage cheese and 1/2 cup cheddar cheese. Spoon about 1/3 cup spinach mixture down the center of each tortilla. Roll up and place seam side down in a 13-in. x 9-in. baking dish coated with cooking spray. Spoon remaining picante sauce over the top.

3 Cover and bake at 350° for 20-25 minutes or until heated through. Uncover; sprinkle with remaining cheese. Bake 5 minutes longer or until cheese is melted.

bacon avocado wraps

PREP/TOTAL TIME: 15 min. | **YIELD:** 4 servings.

A zippy chipotle sauce spikes up the flavor in these fuss-free wraps. To mix things up, feel free to use different varieties of flavored flour tortillas. TASTE OF HOME TEST KITCHEN

- 1/3 cup mayonnaise
- 2 tablespoons chipotle sauce
- 1 tablespoon sour cream
- 1 package (2.1 ounces) ready-to-serve fully cooked bacon
- 4 flour tortillas (8 inches)
- 4 large lettuce leaves
- 1 large tomato, sliced
- 2 medium ripe avocados, peeled and sliced

1 In a small bowl, combine the mayonnaise, chipotle sauce and sour cream until smooth. Heat the bacon according to the package directions.

2 Spread chipotle mayonnaise over tortillas; layer with lettuce, tomato, bacon and avocados. Roll up tightly.

EDITOR'S NOTE: This recipe was tested with San Marcos brand chipotle sauce. It can be found in the Mexican section of your grocery store.

tasty burritos

PREP/TOTAL TIME: 30 min. | **YIELD:** 6 servings.

My cousin is of Mexican heritage, and I've watched her make these crunchy burritos for years. The very first time I made them for my own family, they became an instant favorite! DEBI LANE, CHATTANOOGA, TENNESSEE

- 1 pound lean ground beef (90% lean)
- 1 envelope taco seasoning
- 1 can (16 ounces) refried beans
- 6 flour tortillas (12 inches), warmed
- 1 cup (4 ounces) shredded Colby-Monterey Jack cheese
- 4 teaspoons canola oil

Sour cream and salsa

1 In a large skillet, cook beef over medium heat until no longer pink; drain. Stir in the taco seasoning. In a small saucepan, cook the refried beans over medium-low heat for 2-3 minutes or until heated through.

2 Spoon about 1/3 cup of beans off-center on each tortilla; top with about 2 rounded tablespoons of beef mixture. Sprinkle with cheese. Fold sides and ends of tortilla over filling and roll up.

3 In a large skillet over medium-high heat, brown burritos in oil on all sides. Serve with sour cream and salsa.

tip Save leftovers from different dishes to make a variety of fillings for burritos. Leftover chili, shredded chicken, hash brown potatoes with eggs, or eggs with tomatoes and onion are all tasty variations. Just place the filling of your choice in the middle of a flour tortilla and roll it up.

gourmet deli turkey wraps

PREP/TOTAL TIME: 15 min. | **YIELD:** 6 servings.

These wraps are a staple for my family. They're easy, delicious and can be served for dinner or lunch, or you can slice them for snacking. TAMARA HANSON, BIG LAKE, MINNESOTA

- 2 tablespoons water
- 2 tablespoons red wine vinegar
- 1 tablespoon olive oil
- 1/8 teaspoon pepper
- 3/4 pound sliced deli turkey
- 6 flour tortillas (8 inches), room temperature
- 4 cups spring mix salad greens
- 2 medium pears, peeled and sliced
- 6 tablespoons crumbled blue cheese
- 6 tablespoons dried cranberries
- 1/4 cup chopped walnuts

1 In a small bowl, whisk the water, vinegar, oil and pepper. Divide turkey among tortillas; top with salad greens, pears, cheese, cranberries and walnuts. Drizzle with dressing. Roll up tightly. Secure with toothpicks.

roast beef roll-ups

PREP/TOTAL TIME: 15 min. | **YIELD:** 4 servings.

Quick to make, these party sandwiches are great for tailgating and other events. Serve them in thin slices for an appetizer, or "Reubenize" them by substituting corned beef, sauerkraut, caraway seeds and Thousand Island dressing.
CLARISSA JO SEEGER, COLUMBIANA, OHIO

- 1 package (14 ounces) coleslaw mix
- 3/4 cup coleslaw salad dressing
- 1/2 cup mayonnaise
- 1/4 cup Dijon mustard
- 2 tablespoons cider vinegar
- 2 teaspoons sugar
- 1/2 teaspoon celery seed
- 1 pound thinly sliced deli roast beef
- 4 Italian herb flatbread wraps
- 1/2 pound Swiss cheese, thinly sliced

1 In a small bowl, combine the first seven ingredients. Divide roast beef among flatbread wraps. Top with cheese and coleslaw mixture; roll up tightly.

garden vegetable roll-ups

PREP/TOTAL TIME: 25 min. | **YIELD:** 4 servings.

My husband and I love these light, tasty roll-ups for lunch. The garden-fresh flavor is unbeatable.

BARBARA BLAKE, WEST BRATTLEBORO, VERMONT

- 1/2 cup reduced-fat garlic-herb cheese spread
- 4 flour tortillas (10 inches)
- 1-1/4 cups chopped seeded tomatoes
- 1-1/4 cups julienned fresh spinach
- 3/4 cup chopped sweet red pepper

- 2 bacon strips, cooked and crumbled
- 1/4 teaspoon coarsely ground pepper

1 Spread 2 tablespoons cheese spread over each tortilla. Top with tomatoes, spinach, red pepper, bacon and pepper. Roll up tightly.

chicken lettuce wraps

PREP/TOTAL TIME: 25 min. | **YIELD:** 2 servings.

Bundle up a tasty blend of garden flavors with these delightful wraps. Sweet and hot accents set them apart.
TASTE OF HOME TEST KITCHEN

- 3 tablespoons chicken broth
- 2 tablespoons plus 2 teaspoons reduced-sodium soy sauce, *divided*
- 1 tablespoon sherry *or* additional chicken broth
- 1-1/2 teaspoons cornstarch
- 1/2 pound ground chicken
- 1 teaspoon canola oil
- 1/4 cup shredded carrot
- 1 teaspoon minced fresh gingerroot
- 1/3 cup plum *or* seedless raspberry preserves
- 2 teaspoons hoisin sauce
- 1/8 teaspoon hot pepper sauce
- 1 green onion, thinly sliced
- 4 Bibb *or* Boston lettuce leaves

1 In a small bowl, combine the broth, 2 tablespoons soy sauce, sherry and cornstarch; set aside. In a large skillet, cook chicken in oil over medium heat until meat is no longer pink; drain. Add carrot and ginger; cook and stir for 2-3 minutes or until carrot is tender.

2 Meanwhile, for dipping sauce, combine the preserves, hoisin sauce, pepper sauce and remaining soy sauce; set aside. Stir cornstarch mixture; add to chicken. Cook and stir until thickened, about 2 minutes. Remove from the heat; stir in green onion.

3 Divide chicken mixture among lettuce leaves. Fold lettuce over filling. Serve with dipping sauce.

tortilla turkey sandwiches

PREP/TOTAL TIME: 20 min. | **YIELD:** 4 servings.

I taught my kids to make simple meals as they were growing up, and these pesto turkey tortillas were one of their all-time favorites. LESLIE HEATH, SALT LAKE CITY, UTAH

- 4 ounces cream cheese, softened
- 2 tablespoons mayonnaise
- 1-1/2 teaspoons prepared pesto
- 4 flour tortillas (8 inches), room temperature
- 1 cup shredded lettuce
- 1/2 pound sliced deli smoked turkey
- 3/4 cup chopped tomato
- 1 can (2-1/4 ounces) sliced ripe olives, drained
- 1 cup (4 ounces) shredded Colby-Monterey Jack cheese

1 In a small bowl, beat the cream cheese, mayonnaise and pesto until blended. Spread about 2 tablespoons over each tortilla. Layer with lettuce, turkey, tomato, olives and cheese; roll up. Secure the wraps with toothpicks.

tip If flour tortillas are too stiff to roll into burritos or wraps without tearing, simply place them between two damp microwave-safe paper towels and warm them in the microwave. Check the tortillas every few seconds and remove them when they are soft and pliable.

egg salad roll-ups

PREP/TOTAL TIME: 15 min. | **YIELD:** 2 servings.

I visited Mexico last year and was inspired by the fresh flavor of the food. Tomatillos and limes were widely used, and they add a tangy punch to this egg salad.

SARAH INGLIS, WAPPINGERS FALLS, NEW YORK

- 1/4 cup mayonnaise
- 2 teaspoons minced fresh cilantro
- 1 tablespoon lime juice
- 1/4 teaspoon cayenne pepper, *optional*
- 1/8 teaspoon salt

Dash pepper

- 4 hard-cooked eggs, chopped
- 2 whole wheat tortillas (8 inches)
- 1 medium tomato, thinly sliced
- 1 medium tomatillo, husks removed, rinsed and thinly sliced

1 In large bowl, combine the mayonnaise, cilantro, lime juice, cayenne if desired, salt and pepper. Stir in eggs.

2 Layer tortillas with tomato, tomatillo and egg salad mixture. Fold sides and ends over filling and roll up.

tip Looking for a lower-fat alternative to mayo for egg salad? Simply add a few spoonfuls of low-fat cottage cheese. The texture blends nicely with the egg, and it reduces the amount of mayo needed to achieve spreading consistency.

barbecue chicken burritos

PREP/TOTAL TIME: 30 min. | **YIELD:** 4 servings.

My husband and I love barbecued chicken on buns, so one day he came up with a brilliant idea to try it in wraps. These make a convenient meal as we always have the ingredients on hand. AMY DANDO, APALACHIN, NEW YORK

- 1/2 pound boneless skinless chicken breasts, cut into 1/2-inch cubes
- 1-1/2 cups julienned green peppers
- 1 cup chopped onion
- 4 tablespoons canola oil, *divided*
- 1/2 cup barbecue sauce
- 1-1/2 cups (6 ounces) shredded Mexican cheese blend
- 4 flour tortillas (10 inches), warmed

Lime wedges, sour cream, shredded lettuce and chopped tomatoes, optional

1 In a large skillet, cook the chicken, green peppers and onion in 2 tablespoons oil over medium heat for 6-8 minutes or until chicken juices run clear. Stir in barbecue sauce. Bring to a boil. Reduce heat; simmer for 1-2 minutes or until heated through.

2 Sprinkle cheese down the center of each tortilla; top with chicken mixture. Fold sides and ends over filling and roll up.

3 In a large skillet, brown burritos in remaining oil on all sides over medium heat. Serve with lime wedges, sour cream, lettuce and tomatoes if desired.

southwestern beef tortillas

PREP: 25 min. | **BAKE:** 8-3/4 hours | **YIELD:** 8 servings.

Beef chuck roast makes for a savory filling in these satisfying tortillas. Slowly cooked to perfection, it's treated to an effortless jalapeno-flavored sauce that makes it stand out from the rest. MARIE RIZZIO, INTERLOCHEN, MICHIGAN

- 1   boneless beef chuck roast (2 pounds)
- 1/2 cup water
- 4   large tomatoes, peeled and chopped
- 1   large green pepper, thinly sliced
- 1   medium onion, chopped
- 1   garlic clove, minced
- 1   bay leaf
- 2   tablespoons canola oil
- 3/4 cup ketchup
- 1/2 cup pickled jalapeno slices
- 1   tablespoon juice from pickled jalapeno slices
- 1   tablespoon cider vinegar
- 1   teaspoon salt
- 1/8 teaspoon garlic salt
- 8   flour tortillas (8 inches), warmed

1 Place roast and water in a 3-qt. slow cooker. Cover and cook on low for 8-9 hours or until meat is tender.

2 Remove meat. When cool enough to handle, shred meat with two forks. Skim fat from cooking liquid; set aside 1/2 cup.

3 In a large skillet, cook the tomatoes, green pepper, onion, garlic and bay leaf in oil for 18-22 minutes or until liquid is reduced to 2 tablespoons.

4 Stir in the ketchup, jalapeno slices and juice, vinegar, salt, garlic salt and reserved cooking liquid. Bring to a boil. Stir in shredded beef; heat through. Discard bay leaf. Serve on tortillas.

turkey enchiladas

PREP: 40 min. | **BAKE:** 40 min. | **YIELD:** 8 servings.

My family likes these enchiladas so much, they request a turkey dinner several times a year just so I'll make this dish with the leftovers. I usually double the recipe.
BEVERLY MATTHEWS, PASCO, WASHINGTON

- 3   cups cubed cooked turkey
- 1   cup chicken broth
- 1   cup cooked long grain rice
- 2   plum tomatoes, chopped
- 1   medium onion, chopped
- 1/2 cup canned chopped green chilies
- 1/2 cup sour cream
- 1/4 cup sliced ripe *or* green olives with pimientos
- 1/4 cup minced fresh cilantro
- 1   teaspoon ground cumin
- 8   flour tortillas (10 inches)
- 1   can (28 ounces) green enchilada sauce, *divided*
- 2   cups (8 ounces) shredded Mexican cheese blend, *divided*

1 In a large saucepan, combine the first 10 ingredients. Bring to a boil. Reduce heat; simmer, uncovered, for 20 minutes. Remove from the heat.

2 Place 1/2 cup of the turkey mixture down the center of each tortilla; top each with 1 teaspoon enchilada sauce and 1 tablespoon cheese. Roll up and place seam side down in a greased 13-in. x 9-in. baking dish. Pour remaining enchilada sauce over top; sprinkle with remaining cheese.

3 Cover and bake at 350° for 30 minutes. Uncover; bake 8-10 minutes longer or until bubbly.

cordon bleu stromboli

PREP: 15 min. + rising | **BAKE:** 25 min. | **YIELD:** 6 servings.

This recipe gives you the taste of chicken cordon bleu without all the work. I roll Swiss cheese and deli meats into a swirled sandwich loaf that bakes to a golden brown. My entire gang looks forward to this dinner.

DIANE SCHUELKE, MADISON, MINNESOTA

- 1 loaf (1 pound) frozen bread dough, thawed
- 2 tablespoons butter, softened
- 8 ounces thinly sliced deli ham
- 1/2 cup shredded Swiss cheese
- 5 ounces thinly sliced deli chicken breast

1 On a lightly floured surface, roll dough into a 10-in. x 8-in. rectangle; spread with butter. Top with ham, cheese and chicken. Roll up jelly-roll style, starting with a long side; pinch seam to seal and tuck ends under.

2 Place seam side down on a greased baking sheet. Cover and let rise for 20 minutes. Bake at 350° for 25-30 minutes or until golden brown. Refrigerate leftovers.

speedy lunch roll-ups

PREP/TOTAL TIME: 15 min. | **YIELD:** 2 servings.

This is such a yummy, quick lunch. I served one to my sister, and a week later she told me that her husband and kids couldn't stop raving about them!

MARY ROBERTS, NEW YORK MILLS, MINNESOTA

- 2 tablespoons spreadable garden vegetable cream cheese
- 2 flavored flour tortillas of your choice (8 inches), room temperature
- 3 thin slices deli turkey (1/2 ounce *each*)
- 1/4 cup shredded lettuce
- 2 tablespoons shredded cheddar cheese
- 2 teaspoons finely chopped onion
- 2 teaspoons finely chopped green pepper
- 2 teaspoons chopped ripe olives
- 4 teaspoons ranch salad dressing

1 Spread cream cheese over tortillas. Layer with turkey, lettuce, cheese, onion, green pepper and olives; drizzle with dressing. Roll up tightly; wrap in plastic wrap. Refrigerate until serving.

vegetarian hummus wraps

PREP/TOTAL TIME: 10 min. | **YIELD:** 2 servings.

I created this recipe to sneak more veggies into my family's diet. I'm an on-the-go mom, and these delicious wraps give me energy to keep up with our busy schedule.

AMBER INDRA, THOUSAND OAKS, CALIFORNIA

- 6 tablespoons hummus
- 2 flour tortillas (8 inches), room temperature
- 1/2 cup shredded carrots
- 1 cup fresh baby spinach
- 6 slices tomato
- 2 tablespoons green goddess salad dressing

1 Spread hummus over each tortilla. Layer with carrots, spinach and tomato; drizzle with dressing. Roll up tightly.

chicken caesar tortillas

PREP/TOTAL TIME: 15 min. | **YIELD:** 6 servings.

This classic handheld features tender chicken, Parmesan cheese, chopped Caesar croutons and the perfect amount of dressing. It's great any night of the week.

NANCY PRATT, LONGVIEW, TEXAS

- 3/4 cup fat-free creamy Caesar salad dressing
- 1/4 cup grated Parmesan cheese
- 1/2 teaspoon garlic powder
- 1/4 teaspoon pepper
- 3 cups cubed cooked chicken breast
- 2 cups torn romaine
- 3/4 cup Caesar salad croutons, coarsely chopped
- 6 whole wheat tortillas (8 inches), room temperature

1 In a large bowl, combine the dressing, cheese, garlic powder and pepper. Add the chicken, romaine and croutons. Spoon 2/3 cup chicken mixture down the center of each tortilla; roll up.

manicotti crepes

PREP: 2 hours + chilling | **BAKE:** 45 min. | **YIELD:** 12 servings.

Delicate homemade crepes replace ordinary pasta shells in this cheesy Italian entree. LORI HENRY, ELKHART, INDIANA

- 2 cans (28 ounces each) diced tomatoes, undrained
- 1-1/2 cups finely chopped onion
- 1 can (6 ounces) tomato paste
- 1/3 cup olive oil
- 4 garlic cloves, minced
- 2 tablespoons dried parsley flakes
- 1 tablespoon sugar
- 1 tablespoon salt
- 1 teaspoon minced fresh oregano
- 1 teaspoon minced fresh basil
- 1/4 teaspoon pepper

CREPES:
- 6 eggs
- 1-1/2 cups water
- 1-1/2 cups all-purpose flour
- Dash salt
- 2 tablespoons canola oil, *divided*

FILLING:
- 2 cartons (15 ounces each) ricotta cheese
- 2 cups (8 ounces) shredded part-skim mozzarella cheese
- 1 cup shredded Parmesan cheese
- 2 eggs
- 1 tablespoon dried parsley flakes
- 1 teaspoon salt
- 1/4 teaspoon pepper

1 In a large saucepan; combine the first 11 ingredients. Bring to a boil. Reduce heat; simmer, uncovered, for 1-1/2 to 2 hours or until sauce is reduced to 5 cups, stirring occasionally.

2 Meanwhile, in a large bowl, beat eggs and water. Combine flour and salt; add to egg mixture and mix well. Cover and refrigerate for 1 hour. In another large bowl, combine filling ingredients. Cover and refrigerate.

3 Heat 3/4 teaspoon oil in an 8-in. nonstick skillet. Stir crepe batter; pour a scant 3 tablespoons into center of skillet. Lift and tilt pan to coat bottom evenly. Cook until top appears dry; turn and cook 15-20 seconds longer. Remove to a wire rack. Repeat with remaining batter, using remaining oil as needed. When cool, stack crepes with waxed paper or paper towels in between.

4 Spread about 1/4 cup filling down the center of each crepe; roll up and place 12 crepes in each of two greased 13-in. x 9-in. baking dishes. Spoon sauce over top. Cover and bake at 350° for 45-50 minutes or until a thermometer reads 160°.

tip Here are some pointers for making perfect crepes. Chill the batter for at least 1 hour before using to reduce any air bubbles. Lightly coat the pan with nonstick cooking spray, butter or oil; heat over medium-high. Add a small amount of batter to the hot pan. Tilt the pan to evenly coat the bottom. When the edges are dry and pull away from pan, gently turn; cook the other side. To prevent crepes from sticking before filling, let them cool on a wire rack or waxed paper. Then stack crepes with waxed paper or paper towels in between.

zesty vegetarian tortillas

PREP/TOTAL TIME: 10 min. | **YIELD:** 2 servings.

Colorful and full of flavor, these delightful handhelds are filled with crisp veggies, pepper Jack cheese and a zesty hot sauce. CORI LEHMAN, JACKSON, TENNESSEE

- 2 tablespoons fat-free mayonnaise
- 1 teaspoon lime juice
- 2 to 4 drops Louisiana-style hot sauce
- 2 spinach tortillas *or* flour tortillas of your choice (8 inches), room temperature
- 2 lettuce leaves
- 1/2 medium green pepper, julienned
- 2 slices pepper Jack cheese

1 In a small bowl, combine the mayonnaise, lime juice and hot sauce. Spread over tortillas. Top with lettuce, green pepper and cheese; roll up tightly.

ham and mango wraps

PREP/TOTAL TIME: 25 min. | **YIELD:** 6 servings.

The unique pairing of savory ham and sweet, juicy mango in these luscious wraps makes a cool summer luncheon treat. For extra-fresh flavor, add chopped watercress or parsley. BONNIE AUSTIN, GRENADA, MISSISSIPPI

- 1/3 cup sour cream
- 1/3 cup mayonnaise
- 2 tablespoons minced fresh basil
- 2 tablespoons minced chives
- 1 tablespoon lemon juice
- 1/8 teaspoon salt

- 1/8 teaspoon pepper
- 3 cups cubed fully cooked ham (about 1 pound)
- 2 to 3 medium mangoes, peeled, chopped and patted dry (about 2 cups)
- 6 flour tortillas (10 inches), room temperature

1 In a large bowl, whisk the first seven ingredients. Stir in ham and mangoes. Spoon about 2/3 cup down the center of each tortilla; roll up tightly.

pastrami deli wraps

PREP/TOTAL TIME: 20 min. | **YIELD:** 4 servings.

My hubby can't seem to get enough of these pastrami wraps. I sometimes add horseradish to shake up the flavor. NILA GRAHL, GURNEE, ILLINOIS

- 1/4 cup reduced-fat spreadable cream cheese
- 1/4 cup coarsely chopped roasted sweet red pepper
- 4 spinach tortillas (8 inches), warmed
- 4 lettuce leaves
- 4 slices deli pastrami
- 4 slices reduced-fat provolone cheese
- 1/4 cup thinly sliced red onion
- 1 small sweet red pepper, julienned
- 1/2 cup chopped cucumber

1 Place cream cheese and roasted pepper in a small food processor. Cover and process until blended. Spread over tortillas. Layer with remaining ingredients; roll up. Secure with toothpicks.

guacamole chicken roll-ups

PREP/TOTAL TIME: 10 min. | **YIELD:** 2 servings.

Seasoned chicken, guacamole and salsa add finger-lickin' Southwest flavor to these zesty roll-ups.

TASTE OF HOME TEST KITCHEN

- 1/4 cup guacamole
- 2 spinach tortillas (8 inches), room temperature
- 1/4 cup salsa
- 1/2 cup shredded Mexican cheese blend
- 1 package (6 ounces) ready-to-use Southwestern chicken strips
- 2 lettuce leaves

1 Spread guacamole over half of each tortilla. Layer with salsa, cheese, chicken and lettuce to within 2 in. of edges. Roll up the tortillas tightly.

california wraps

PREP/TOTAL TIME: 15 min. | **YIELD:** 4 servings.

Hummus is a fantastic health-conscious alternative to mayonnaise. The combination of fresh ingredients makes these so good. DONNA MUNCH, EL PASO, TEXAS

- 1/3 cup prepared hummus
- 4 whole wheat tortillas (8 inches)
- 2 cups cubed cooked chicken breast
- 1/4 cup chopped roasted sweet red peppers

- 1/4 cup crumbled feta cheese
- 1/4 cup thinly sliced fresh basil leaves

1 Spread hummus on tortillas; top with chicken, peppers, cheese and basil. Roll up.

avocado tomato wraps

PREP/TOTAL TIME: 10 min. | **YIELD:** 2 servings.

I eat these super-fast wrap sandwiches all summer long. The creamy avocado and sweet tomato never fail to satisfy. It doesn't get more simple and delicious than this!

MEGAN WISENER, MILWAUKEE, WISCONSIN

- 1 medium ripe avocado, peeled and thinly sliced
- 2 flavored tortillas of your choice (10 inches), room temperature
- 2 lettuce leaves
- 1 medium tomato, thinly sliced
- 2 tablespoons shredded Parmesan cheese
- 1/4 teaspoon garlic powder
- 1/8 teaspoon salt
- 1/8 teaspoon pepper

1 In a small bowl, mash a fourth of the avocado with a fork; spread over tortillas. Layer with lettuce, tomato and remaining avocado. Sprinkle with cheese, garlic powder, salt and pepper; roll up. Serve wraps immediately.

weeknight catfish wraps

PREP: 10 min. + chilling | **COOK:** 10 min. | **YIELD:** 2 servings.

I tuck catfish nuggets and a convenient coleslaw mix into tortilla wraps with tasty results. They're an easy way to help us get more fish in our diet.

MONICA PERRY, BOISE, IDAHO

- 1-1/2 cups coleslaw mix
- 2 tablespoons finely chopped onion
- 1/8 teaspoon pepper
- 1 teaspoon Cajun *or* Creole seasoning, *divided*
- 1/4 cup coleslaw salad dressing
- 2 tablespoons pancake mix
- 1/2 pound catfish fillets, cut into 2-inch pieces
- 1 teaspoon canola oil
- 4 flour tortillas (6 inches), warmed

1 In a small bowl, combine the coleslaw mix, onion, pepper and 1/4 teaspoon seasoning. Stir in dressing. Cover and refrigerate for at least 30 minutes.

2 In a resealable plastic bag, combine the pancake mix and remaining seasoning. Add fish and toss to coat. In a small skillet, cook fish in oil over medium heat for 6 minutes or until lightly browned on each side and fish flakes easily with a fork. Spoon coleslaw mixture onto tortillas; top with fish and roll up.

chicken tortillas

PREP/TOTAL TIME: 10 min. | **YIELD:** 4 servings.

Use your favorite flavor of cheese spread and tortillas to wrap up this filling sandwich. You can serve any extra spread with vegetables as a side dish.

MARGIE HAEN, MENOMONEE FALLS, WISCONSIN

- 1/2 cup garlic-herb cheese spread
- 4 flavored flour tortillas of your choice (8 inches), room temperature
- 4 large lettuce leaves
- 3 plum tomatoes, cut into thin slices
- 1 package (6 ounces) thinly sliced deli smoked chicken breast
- 1 medium cucumber, cut lengthwise into thin slices
- 1/2 cup shredded carrot

1 Spread 2 tablespoons of cheese spread over each tortilla. Layer with the lettuce, tomatoes, chicken, cucumber and carrot. Roll up tightly.

tip You can find Cajun seasoning in the spice section of your grocery store. You can also make your own. Although there are many different blends, a typical mix includes salt, onion powder, garlic powder, cayenne pepper, ground mustard, celery seed and pepper.

shredded pork burritos

PREP: 25 min. | **BAKE:** 9 hours | **YIELD:** 16 servings (2-1/3 cups sauce).

Pork roast is slow-cooked with sweet and savory ingredients, including a can of cola, to create tender, shredded pork burritos. A tomatillo sauce, made with an easy dressing mix, tops it all off for an out-of-this-world entree.

KATHERINE NELSON, CENTERVILLE, UTAH

1 bone-in pork shoulder roast (5 pounds)
2 tablespoons plus 1/2 cup packed brown sugar, *divided*
4 teaspoons paprika, *divided*
2 teaspoons crushed red pepper flakes
2 teaspoons ground cumin
1 teaspoon salt
1 can (12 ounces) cola
1 cup chicken broth
1 large sweet onion, thinly sliced
2 garlic cloves, minced

TOMATILLO SAUCE:

1 cup mayonnaise
1/2 cup 2% milk
2 tomatillos, husks removed
3/4 cup fresh cilantro leaves
1 jalapeno pepper, seeded and cut into chunks
1 envelope ranch salad dressing mix
1 tablespoon lime juice
1 garlic clove, peeled
1/8 teaspoon cayenne pepper
16 flour tortillas (8 inches), room temperature

1 Cut the roast in half. Combine 2 tablespoons brown sugar, 2 teaspoons paprika, pepper flakes, cumin and salt; rub over meat. Place in a 4-qt. slow cooker. Add the cola, broth, onion and garlic. Cover and cook on low for 8-10 hours or until meat is tender.

2 Set meat aside until cool enough to handle. Remove meat from bones; discard bones. Shred meat with two forks. Skim fat from cooking juices and return meat to slow cooker. Stir in remaining brown sugar and paprika. Cover and cook on low for 1 hour or until heated through.

3 Meanwhile, in a blender, combine the mayonnaise, milk, tomatillos, cilantro, jalapeno, dressing mix, lime juice, garlic and cayenne. Cover and process until blended. Pour into a small bowl. Chill until serving.

4 Using a slotted spoon, spoon 1/2 cup filling off center on each tortilla. Drizzle with some of the tomatillo sauce. Fold sides and ends over filling and roll up. Serve with remaining sauce.

EDITOR'S NOTE: Wear disposable gloves when cutting hot peppers; the oils can burn skin. Avoid touching your face.

SAUSAGE & SPINACH CALZONES, PG. 86

pitas & pockets

REUBEN BRAIDS, PG. 94

MANGO SHRIMP PITAS, PG. 91

beef gyros

PREP/TOTAL TIME: 30 min. | **YIELD:** 5 servings.

Going out to restaurants for gyros started to add up, so I came up with this budget-friendly homemade version. Now my hubby and kids request them all the time. I set out the fixings so we can assemble our own.
SHERI SCHEERHORN, HILLS, MINNESOTA

- 1 cup ranch salad dressing
- 1/2 cup chopped seeded peeled cucumber
- 1 pound beef top sirloin steak, cut into thin strips
- 2 tablespoons olive oil
- 5 whole pita breads, warmed
- 1 medium tomato, chopped
- 1 can (2-1/4 ounces) sliced ripe olives, drained
- 1/2 small onion, thinly sliced
- 1 cup (4 ounces) crumbled feta cheese
- 2-1/2 cups shredded lettuce

1 In a small bowl, combine salad dressing and cucumber; set aside. In a large skillet, cook beef in oil over medium heat until no longer pink.

2 Layer half of each pita with steak, tomato, olives, onion, cheese, lettuce and dressing mixture. Fold each pita over filling; secure with toothpicks.

hawaiian ham salad pockets

PREP/TOTAL TIME: 15 min. | **YIELD:** 4 servings.

Looking for a great way to use up leftover ham? Try these sandwiches. The flavors of pineapple and mustard are the perfect complement to the savory meat.
MITZI SENTIFF, ANNAPOLIS, MARYLAND

- 1-1/4 cups cubed fully cooked lean ham
- 3/4 cup unsweetened pineapple tidbits
- 1 large carrot, chopped
- 1/4 cup fat-free mayonnaise
- 1 tablespoon honey mustard
- 2 pita breads (6 inches), halved
- 4 lettuce leaves

1 In a small bowl, combine the ham, pineapple and carrot. Stir in the mayonnaise and mustard until blended. Line each pita half with a lettuce leaf; fill with ham salad.

lunch-box "handwiches"

PREP/TOTAL TIME: 15 min. | **YIELD:** 10 servings.

Forget ho-hum ham and cheese sandwiched between bread. Kids will go crazy for these pockets oozing with the classic lunchtime ingredients. CALLIE MYERS, ROCKPORT, TEXAS

- 1 loaf (1 pound) frozen bread dough, thawed
- 2-1/2 cups finely chopped fully cooked ham
- 1 cup (4 ounces) shredded Swiss cheese
- 1 egg yolk
- 1 tablespoon water

1 Let dough rise according to package directions. Punch down; divide into 10 pieces. On a lightly floured surface, roll each piece into a 5-in. circle. Place one circle on a greased baking sheet.

2 Place about 1/4 cup ham and 2 tablespoons cheese to within 1/2 in. of edges; press filling to flatten. Combine egg yolk and water; brush edges of dough with egg yolk mixture. Fold dough over filling and pinch edges to seal. Repeat with remaining dough and filling. Brush tops with remaining egg yolk mixture.

3 Bake at 375° for 15-20 minutes or until golden brown. Serve warm or cold. If desired, cool and freeze.

baked chicken chimichangas

PREP: 20 min. | **BAKE:** 20 min. | **YIELD:** 6 servings.

I developed this quick and easy sensation through trial and error. I used to garnish the chimichangas with sour cream, but eliminated it to lighten the recipe. My friends can't seem to get enough, and we all appreciate that these are much healthier than their deep-fried counterparts.
RICKEY MADDEN, CLINTON, SOUTH CAROLINA

1-1/2 cups cubed cooked chicken breast
1-1/2 cups picante sauce, *divided*
  1/2 cup shredded reduced-fat cheddar cheese
  2/3 cup chopped green onions, *divided*
   1 teaspoon ground cumin
   1 teaspoon dried oregano
   6 flour tortillas (8 inches), warmed
   1 tablespoon butter, melted

1 In a small bowl, combine the chicken, 3/4 cup picante sauce, cheese, 1/4 cup onions, cumin and oregano. Spoon 1/2 cup mixture down the center of each tortilla. Fold sides and ends over filling and roll up. Place seam side down in a 15-in. x 10-in. x 1-in. baking pan coated with cooking spray. Brush with butter.

2 Bake, uncovered, at 375° for 20-25 minutes or until heated through. Top with remaining picante sauce and onions.

zesty tacos

PREP/TOTAL TIME: 30 min. | **YIELD:** 8 servings.

Jazz up everyday tacos in a snap. Black-eyed peas and a drizzle of Italian dressing are the surprise ingredients that perk up this recipe. SUSIE BONHAM, FAIRVIEW, OKLAHOMA

   1 pound lean ground beef (90% lean)
   1 cup water
   1 envelope taco seasoning
   8 taco shells
   1 can (15-1/2 ounces) black-eyed peas, rinsed and drained
   1 cup chopped tomatoes
   1 cup shredded lettuce
   1 cup (4 ounces) shredded cheddar cheese
  1/2 cup zesty Italian salad dressing

1 In a large skillet, cook beef over medium heat for 5-6 minutes or until meat is no longer pink; drain. Stir in water and taco seasoning. Bring to a boil. Reduce heat; simmer, uncovered, for 4-5 minutes or until thickened.

2 Meanwhile, prepare taco shells according to package directions. Stir peas into skillet; heat through. Spoon 1/4 cup beef mixture into each taco shell. Top with tomatoes, lettuce and cheese. Drizzle with salad dressing.

> **tip** On a day when you have the time, crumble and brown several pounds of ground beef. Drain and spread on a baking sheet. Freeze until solid. Transfer to freezer bags in 1/2- or 1-pound amounts. On busy days, pull out a bag and add to tacos or any recipe that uses browned ground beef.

fruited turkey salad pitas

PREP: 30 min. + chilling | **YIELD:** 8 servings.

Give leftover turkey gets a great makeover in this tasty spread that feeds a crowd. Apples, pecans and celery give the delightful salad a nice crunch. DONNA NOEL, GRAY, MAINE

- 1/2 cup reduced-fat plain yogurt
- 1/2 cup reduced-fat mayonnaise
-   2 tablespoons lemon juice
- 1/2 teaspoon pepper
-   4 cups cubed cooked turkey breast
-   2 celery ribs, thinly sliced
-   1 medium apple, peeled and chopped
- 1/2 cup finely chopped fresh spinach
- 1/3 cup dried cranberries
- 1/3 cup chopped pecans
-   8 pita breads (6 inches), halved
- 16 romaine leaves
-   8 slices red onion, separated into rings

1 In a small bowl, combine the yogurt, mayonnaise, lemon juice and pepper. In a large bowl, combine the turkey, celery, apple, spinach, cranberries and pecans. Add yogurt mixture and stir to coat. Cover and refrigerate until chilled.

2 Line pita halves with lettuce and onion; fill each with 1/2 cup turkey mixture.

sweet 'n' sour pockets

PREP: 10 min. + chilling | **YIELD:** 5 servings.

This recipe boasts classic sweet and sour flavors. My family requests it often. KATHY HARRIS, OLD HICKORY, TENNESSEE

- 1/3 cup mayonnaise
- 1/3 cup sour cream
- 1/2 teaspoon Dijon mustard

- 3/4 cup pineapple tidbits, drained
-   5 pita pocket breads (6 inches), halved
- 10 lettuce leaves
- 10 slices (1 ounce *each*) fully cooked ham
- 1/2 cup chopped green pepper
- 1/2 cup chopped red onion

1 In a small bowl, combine the mayonnaise, sour cream and mustard. Cover and chill for 1 hour.

2 Just before serving, stir in the pineapple. Fill each pita half with lettuce, ham, 2 tablespoons pineapple mixture, green pepper and onion.

crab salad pockets

PREP/TOTAL TIME: 15 min. | **YIELD:** 1 serving.

These pockets make a tasty, light lunch. If you don't have crabmeat on hand, you can replace it with tuna for great results. PENNY BOKOVOY, ULM, MONTANA

-   2 ounces imitation crabmeat, flaked *or* canned crabmeat, drained, flaked and cartilage removed
- 1/4 cup finely chopped cucumber
-   2 tablespoons chopped sweet red pepper
-   2 tablespoons chopped green pepper
-   1 tablespoon sliced green onion
-   1 tablespoon finely chopped celery
- 1/4 teaspoon seafood seasoning
-   2 tablespoons mayonnaise
-   2 whole wheat pita pocket halves

1 In a large bowl, combine the crab, cucumber, peppers, onion, celery and seafood seasoning. Stir in mayonnaise. Fill pita halves with crab mixture.

pear waldorf pitas

PREP: 10 min. + chilling | **YIELD:** 10 servings.

Here's a guaranteed table-brightener for a shower, luncheon or party. Just stand back and watch these sandwiches vanish. For an eye-catching presentation, tuck each one into a colorful folded napkin.

ROXANN PARKER, DOVER, DELAWARE

- 2 medium ripe pears, diced
- 1/2 cup thinly sliced celery
- 1/2 cup halved seedless red grapes
- 2 tablespoons finely chopped walnuts
- 2 tablespoons lemon yogurt
- 2 tablespoons mayonnaise
- 1/8 teaspoon poppy seeds
- 10 miniature pita pockets, halved

Lettuce leaves

1 In a large bowl, combine the pears, celery, grapes and walnuts. In another bowl, whisk the yogurt, mayonnaise and poppy seeds. Add to pear mixture; toss to coat. Refrigerate for 1 hour or overnight.

2 Line pita halves with lettuce; fill each with 2 tablespoons pear mixture.

flatbread tacos with ranch sour cream

PREP/TOTAL TIME: 30 min. | **YIELD:** 8 servings.

These tasty flatbread tacos, made with convenient refrigerated biscuits, are ideal for serving buffet-style. Set out the toppings and let everyone assemble their own!

JENNIFER EGGEBRAATEN, BOTHELL, WASHINGTON

- 1 cup (8 ounces) sour cream
- 2 teaspoons ranch salad dressing mix
- 1 teaspoon lemon juice
- 1-1/2 pounds ground beef
- 1 can (15 ounces) pinto beans, rinsed and drained
- 1 can (14-1/2 ounces) diced tomatoes, undrained
- 1 envelope taco seasoning
- 1 tablespoon hot pepper sauce
- 1 tube (16.3 ounces) large refrigerated buttermilk biscuits

Optional toppings: sliced ripe olives and shredded lettuce and cheddar cheese

1 In a small bowl, combine the sour cream, dressing mix and lemon juice; chill until serving.

2 In a large skillet, cook beef over medium heat until no longer pink; drain. Add the beans, tomatoes, taco seasoning and pepper sauce; heat through.

3 Meanwhile, roll out each biscuit into a 6-in. circle. In a small nonstick skillet over medium heat, cook each biscuit for 30-60 seconds on each side or until golden brown; keep warm.

4 To serve, spread each flatbread with 2 tablespoons ranch sour cream; top each with 2/3 cup meat mixture. Sprinkle with toppings if desired.

portobello pockets

PREP: 30 min. + marinating | **COOK:** 10 min. | **YIELD:** 8 servings.

This savory recipe is one of my favorites. It's quick, easy and filled with a bounty of fresh veggies. I vary the produce and spices to fit the season. For fuss-free hikes or picnics, bundle up Portobello Pockets in foil, then take them along to toss on a hot grill. ELISSA ARMBRUSTER, MEDFORD, NEW JERSEY

1/4 cup water

3 tablespoons lime juice

2 tablespoons canola oil

1 tablespoon Italian seasoning

1 teaspoon dried minced garlic

1/2 teaspoon dried celery flakes

1/4 teaspoon salt

1/4 teaspoon ground cumin

1/4 teaspoon ground nutmeg

1/4 teaspoon pepper

1/8 teaspoon cayenne pepper

1 pound sliced baby portobello mushrooms

1 *each* medium sweet yellow and red pepper, thinly sliced

1 medium red onion, thinly sliced

2 small zucchini, cut into 1/4-inch slices

1 cup (4 ounces) shredded reduced-fat Mexican cheese blend

8 pita breads (6 inches), cut in half

1 In a large resealable bag, combine the first 11 ingredients. Add the mushrooms, peppers, onion and zucchini; seal bag and turn to coat. Refrigerate overnight.

2 In a large nonstick skillet coated with cooking spray, cook and stir the vegetable mixture over medium-high heat for 6-8 minutes or until crisp-tender. Stir in cheese; cook 2-3 minutes longer or until cheese is melted. Stuff each pita half with 1/2 cup vegetable-cheese mixture.

sausage & spinach calzones

PREP/TOTAL TIME: 30 min. | **YIELD:** 4 servings.

These are perfect for quick lunches or a midnight snack. My nurse coworkers always ask me to make them when it's my turn to bring in lunch.

KOURTNEY WILLIAMS, MECHANICSVILLE, VIRGINIA

 1/2   pound bulk Italian sausage
 1   tube (13.8 ounces) refrigerated pizza crust
 3/4   cup shredded part-skim mozzarella cheese
 2-2/3   cups fresh baby spinach
 1/2   cup part-skim ricotta cheese
 1/4   teaspoon salt
 1/4   teaspoon pepper

1 In a large skillet, cook sausage over medium heat until no longer pink. Meanwhile, unroll pizza crust; pat into a 15-in. x 11-in. rectangle. Cut into four rectangles. Sprinkle mozzarella cheese over half of each rectangle to within 1 in. of edges.

2 Drain sausage. Add spinach; cook and stir over medium heat until spinach is wilted. Remove from the heat. Stir in the ricotta cheese, salt and pepper; spread over mozzarella cheese. Fold dough over filling; press edges with a fork to seal.

3 Transfer to a greased baking sheet. Bake at 400° for 10-15 minutes or until lightly browned.

black bean 'n' corn quesadillas

PREP/TOTAL TIME: 25 min. | **YIELD:** 6 servings.

Black beans partner up with spinach and corn in these easy and satisfying Southwestern quesadillas.

SUSAN FRANKLIN, LITTLETON, COLORADO

 1   can (15 ounces) black beans, rinsed and drained, *divided*
 1   small onion, finely chopped
 2   teaspoons olive oil
 1   can (11 ounces) Mexicorn, drained
 1   teaspoon chili powder
 1   teaspoon ground cumin
 1   package (6 ounces) fresh baby spinach
 8   flour tortillas (8 inches)
 3/4   cup shredded reduced-fat Monterey Jack cheese *or* Mexican cheese blend

1 In a small bowl, mash 1 cup beans with a fork. In a large skillet, saute onion in oil until tender. Add the corn, chili powder, cumin, mashed beans and remaining beans; cook and stir until heated through. Stir in spinach just until wilted.

2 Place two tortillas on an ungreased baking sheet; spread each with a rounded 1/2 cup of bean mixture. Sprinkle each with 3 tablespoons of cheese; top with another tortilla. Repeat.

3 Bake at 400° for 8-10 minutes or until cheese is melted. Cut each quesadilla into six wedges. Serve warm.

sesame hot dogs

PREP/TOTAL TIME: 30 min. | **YIELD:** 8 servings.

Kids of all ages love these cute, cheese-stuffed hot dogs wrapped in crusty, sesame-seed biscuits. I serve them with bowls of chili, mustard, ketchup—even bean dip or salsa for dipping. SUE MACKEY, JACKSON, WISCONSIN

 8   hot dogs
 1/4   cup sharp American cheese spread
 1   tube (16.3 ounces) large refrigerated buttermilk biscuits
 2   tablespoons butter, melted
 1/4   cup sesame seeds

1 Make a lengthwise slit three-quarters of the way through each hot dog to within 1/2 in. of each end. Spread cheese into pockets. Roll each biscuit into a 5-in. circle; wrap one around each hot dog. Brush with butter and roll in sesame seeds.

2 Place on a lightly greased baking sheet. Bake at 425° for 11-13 minutes or until golden brown.

cheeseburger pockets

PREP: 30 min. | **BAKE:** 10 min. | **YIELD:** 5 servings.

I love cooking with ground beef because it's versatile, flavorful and economical. Refrigerated biscuits save you the trouble of making dough from scratch.

PAT CHAMBLESS, CROWDER, OKLAHOMA

- 1/2 pound lean ground beef (90% lean)
- 1 tablespoon chopped onion
- 1/2 teaspoon salt
- 1/8 teaspoon pepper
- 1 tube (12 ounces) refrigerated buttermilk biscuits
- 5 slices process American cheese

1 In a large skillet, cook the beef, onion, salt and pepper over medium heat until meat is no longer pink; drain and cool.

2 Place two biscuits overlapping on a floured surface; roll out into a 5-in. oval. Place 3 tablespoons meat mixture on one side. Fold a cheese slice to fit over meat mixture. Fold dough over filling; press edges with a fork to seal. Repeat with remaining biscuits, meat mixture and cheese.

3 Place on a greased baking sheet. Prick tops with a fork. Bake at 400° for 10 minutes or until golden brown.

EDITOR'S NOTE: Pricking the tops of Cheeseburger Pockets helps steam escape during baking. If you don't do this, the pockets will puff up and may break open.

tip Use your blender to chop onions quickly. Quarter the onions, place in the blender and cover with water. Cover and process on high speed for two seconds or until chopped. Pour into a colander to drain and add to recipe as instructed.

sloppy joe calzones

PREP: 20 min. | **BAKE:** 15 min. | **YIELD:** 4 servings.

It's a kid-friendly Friday night with these simple calzones. Chop the onion and pepper super-fine for your really picky eaters. TASTE OF HOME TEST KITCHEN

- 1 pound ground beef
- 1 cup chopped onion
- 1 cup chopped green pepper
- 1 can (15 ounces) black beans, rinsed and drained
- 1 can (6 ounces) tomato paste
- 1/2 cup water
- 1/2 cup ketchup
- 1 teaspoon dried oregano
- 1/4 teaspoon salt
- 2 tubes (8 ounces *each*) refrigerated crescent rolls
- 1 cup (4 ounces) shredded cheddar cheese

1 In a large skillet, cook the beef, onion and pepper over medium heat until meat is no longer pink; drain. Stir in the beans, tomato paste, water, ketchup, oregano and salt.

2 Separate crescent dough into four rectangles; seal perforations. Spoon a fourth of the meat mixture onto half of each rectangle; sprinkle with cheese. Fold dough over filling; pinch edges to seal. Cut slits in tops.

3 Place on an ungreased baking sheet. Bake at 375° for 13-15 minutes or until golden brown.

fast fajita pita

PREP/TOTAL TIME: 15 min. | **YIELD:** 2 servings.

These zippy fajitas are perfect for busy days when you don't have a lot of time to spend in the kitchen. I like to serve them for lunch with carrot sticks, pickle spears and my favorite chips. CATHY BELL, JOPLIN, MISSOURI

- 1/2 medium onion, sliced
- 1/2 medium sweet red *or* green pepper, julienned
- 1-1/2 teaspoons fajita seasoning
- 1 tablespoon olive oil
- 2 slices deli roast beef, julienned
- 2 slices Monterey Jack cheese (1/2 ounce *each*)
- 4 lettuce leaves
- 2 pita breads (6 inches), halved and warmed
- 1/2 medium tomato, diced
- 2 tablespoons salsa, optional
- 2 tablespoons prepared ranch salad dressing, optional

1 In a small skillet, saute the onion, red pepper and fajita seasoning in oil until vegetables are just tender. Add roast beef; saute 5-6 minutes longer or until beef is heated through.

2 Place a piece of cheese and a lettuce leaf in each pita half; fill with beef mixture and tomato. Serve with salsa and ranch dressing.

tip Olive oil can be stored tightly capped at room temperature or in the refrigerator for up to 1 year. When chilled, the oil turns cloudy and thick. Chilled olive oil will return to its original consistency when left at room temperature for a short time.

barbecued chicken quesadillas

PREP/TOTAL TIME: 30 min. | **YIELD:** 2 servings.

I jazz up everyday quesadillas with barbecue sauce, then top things off with a sweet and spicy mango salsa.
HEIDI VAWDREY, RIVERTON, UTAH

- 1 medium mango, peeled and diced
- 2 small plum tomatoes, seeded and diced
- 1/3 cup diced green pepper
- 3 green onions, chopped
- 3 tablespoons minced fresh cilantro
- 1 small Anaheim *or* jalapeno pepper, seeded and diced
- 3 tablespoons lime juice

Salt and pepper to taste

QUESADILLAS:

- 1 tablespoon butter, softened
- 2 flour tortillas (8 inches)
- 3/4 cup shredded cheddar-Monterey Jack cheese
- 1 cup chopped cooked chicken breast
- 1/4 cup barbecue sauce

1 In a small bowl, combine the first nine ingredients; cover and refrigerate.

2 Spread butter over one side of each tortilla. Place tortillas, buttered side down, on griddle. Sprinkle one side of each tortilla with 3 tablespoons cheese. Combine chicken and barbecue sauce; spoon over cheese. Sprinkle with remaining cheese.

3 Fold over and cook over low heat for 1-2 minutes on each side or until cheese is melted. Cut into wedges. Serve with salsa.

EDITOR'S NOTE: Wear disposable gloves when cutting hot peppers; the oils can burn skin. Avoid touching your face.

chili pockets

PREP/TOTAL TIME: 25 min. | **YIELD:** 4 servings.

Bring some fun to the table with this scrumptious twist on chili. Made with just a few basic ingredients, these pockets offer a family-friendly meal in no time.

DIANE ANGELL, ROCKFORD, ILLINOIS

- 1 can (15 ounces) chili with beans
- 1/2 cup shredded cheddar cheese
- 2 tablespoons minced fresh cilantro
- 1 can (13.8 ounces) refrigerated pizza crust
- 4-1/2 teaspoons cornmeal, *divided*

Sour cream and salsa

1 In a small bowl, combine the chili, cheese and cilantro. Roll pizza dough into a 12-in. square; cut into four 6-in. squares. Spoon 1/2 cup chili mixture onto the center of each square; brush edges of dough with water. Fold one corner of each square over filling to the opposite corner, forming a triangle. Using a fork, crimp edges to seal.

2 Sprinkle 1-1/2 teaspoons cornmeal over a greased 15-in. x 10-in. x 1-in. baking pan. Place pockets in pan; prick tops with a fork. Sprinkle with remaining cornmeal.

3 Bake at 425° for 10-12 minutes or until golden brown. Serve with sour cream and salsa.

seafood salad pitas

PREP: 20 min. + chilling | **YIELD:** 8 servings.

This tasty and colorful sandwich makes a great light lunch.

LINDA EVANCOE-COBLE, LEOLA, PENNSYLVANIA

- 2 cups chopped imitation crabmeat (about 10 ounces)
- 1/2 pound cooked medium shrimp, peeled, deveined and chopped (about 1 cup)

- 2 celery ribs, chopped
- 1/2 cup thinly sliced green onions
- 3/4 cup fat-free mayonnaise
- 3/4 teaspoon seafood seasoning
- 1/4 teaspoon salt
- 1/8 teaspoon pepper
- 8 whole wheat pita pocket halves

1 In a large bowl, combine the crab, shrimp, celery and onions. In a small bowl, combine the mayonnaise, seafood seasoning, salt and pepper. Pour over crab mixture; toss to coat. Cover and refrigerate for at least 2 hours. Spoon into pita halves.

greek chicken sandwiches

PREP/TOTAL TIME: 25 min. | **YIELD:** 4 servings.

My wife and I enjoyed sandwiches similar to these at a restaurant. I decided to try my hand at my own version that I think is even more flavorful and zesty...and easier to make, too! TOM WOLF, TIGARD, OREGON

- 1 pound boneless skinless chicken breasts, cut into 1-inch cubes
- 1/3 cup fat-free creamy Caesar salad dressing
- 1/4 cup crumbled feta cheese
- 1/4 cup pitted Greek olives, finely chopped
- 1/4 teaspoon garlic powder
- 4 pita breads (6 inches), halved
- 8 lettuce leaves
- 1 medium tomato, sliced
- 1 small onion, sliced

1 In a large nonstick skillet coated with cooking spray, cook and stir chicken over medium heat until no longer pink. Add the dressing, cheese, olives and garlic powder; heat through.

2 Line pita halves with lettuce, tomato and onion; fill each with about 1/3 cup chicken mixture.

zucchini pizza loaves

PREP: 30 min. | **BAKE:** 30 min. | **YIELD:** 2 loaves (4 servings each).

Full of good-for-you veggies, these loaves taste like indulgent pizzas—even picky eaters go back for seconds. In summer, I assemble and freeze several to serve at winter potlucks and parties. TRISHA KRUSE, EAGLE, IDAHO

- 2 medium zucchini, thinly sliced
- 1 medium onion, finely chopped
- 1 cup sliced fresh mushrooms
- 2 teaspoons olive oil
- 2 garlic cloves, minced
- 1 can (8 ounces) no-salt-added tomato sauce
- 1 medium tomato, seeded and chopped
- 1 can (2-1/4 ounces) sliced ripe olives, drained
- 2 teaspoons Italian seasoning
- 2 tubes (11 ounces *each*) refrigerated crusty French loaf
- 3 slices provolone cheese, chopped
- 1 ounce sliced turkey pepperoni, julienned
- 1 cup (4 ounces) shredded part-skim mozzarella cheese

1 In a large skillet, saute the zucchini, onion, mushrooms in oil until tender. Add garlic; cook 1 minute longer. Stir in the tomato sauce, tomato, olives and Italian seasoning; remove from the heat.

2 Unroll one loaf of dough, starting at the seam. Pat into a 14-in. x 12-in. rectangle. Sprinkle half of the provolone and pepperoni to within 1/2 in. of edges. Spread with half of the zucchini mixture; sprinkle with half of the mozzarella.

3 Roll up jelly-roll style, starting with a long side; pinch seams to seal. Place seam side down on a baking sheet coated with cooking spray. Repeat with remaining dough, pepperoni, cheeses and zucchini mixture.

4 Bake at 350° for 30-35 minutes or until golden brown. Slice and serve warm.

mango shrimp pitas

PREP: 15 min. + marinating | **GRILL:** 10 min. | **YIELD:** 4 servings.

Mango, ginger and curry combine with a splash of lime juice to coat juicy grilled shrimp. Stuffed in pitas, the shrimp combo makes for a delectable hand-held entree. You can also serve it atop a bed of rice for a less casual presentation. BEVERLY OFERRALL, LINKWOOD, MARYLAND

- 1/2 cup mango chutney
- 3 tablespoons lime juice
- 1 teaspoon grated fresh gingerroot
- 1/2 teaspoon curry powder
- 1 pound uncooked large shrimp, peeled and deveined
- 2 pita breads (6 inches), halved
- 8 Bibb *or* Boston lettuce leaves
- 1 large tomato, thinly sliced

1 In a small bowl, combine the chutney, lime juice, ginger and curry. Pour 1/2 cup marinade into a large resealable plastic bag; add the shrimp. Seal bag and turn to coat; refrigerate for at least 15 minutes. Cover and refrigerate remaining marinade.

2 Drain and discard marinade. Thread shrimp onto four metal or soaked wooden skewers. Moisten a paper towel with cooking oil; using long-handled tongs, lightly coat the grill rack.

3 Grill shrimp, covered, over medium heat or broil 4 in. from the heat for 6-8 minutes or until shrimp turn pink, turning frequently.

4 Fill pita halves with lettuce, tomato and shrimp; spoon reserved chutney mixture over filling.

ham and cheese calzones

PREP: 20 min. | **BAKE:** 20 min.
YIELD: 2 calzones (7 servings each).

I concocted this inside-out pizza one evening when I had leftover baked ham and needed to fix something quick. Everyone loved it! SHELBY MARINO, NEPTUNE BEACH, FLORIDA

- 2 tubes (13.8 ounces *each*) refrigerated pizza crust
- 1 cup ricotta cheese
- 4 to 6 ounces sliced pepperoni
- 2 cups diced fully cooked ham
- 2 cups (8 ounces) shredded part-skim mozzarella cheese

Shredded Parmesan cheese, optional
Dried basil, optional
Meatless spaghetti sauce, warmed

1 Unroll one pizza crust on a greased baking sheet; roll out into a 14-in. x 11-in. rectangle. Spread half of the ricotta cheese lengthwise on half of the dough to within 1 in. of the edges.

2 Sprinkle with half of the pepperoni, ham and mozzarella cheese. Fold dough over filling; press edges firmly to seal. Repeat with remaining crust and filling ingredients.

3 Bake at 400° for 20-25 minutes or until golden brown. Sprinkle with Parmesan cheese and basil if desired. Cut into slices. Serve with spaghetti sauce.

giant calzone

PREP: 25 min. + rising | **BAKE:** 40 min. | **YIELD:** 6 servings.

The filling ingredients inside this impressive calzone are our personal favorites, but feel free to substitute others of your choice. We use the extra sauce for dipping or freeze it for later. You can also make two smaller calzones instead of a single large one. RONNA ANDERSON, PRAGUE, OKLAHOMA

- 1-1/2 cups water (70° to 80°)
- 2 tablespoons olive oil
- 2 teaspoons sugar
- 2 teaspoons salt
- 4-1/2 cups all-purpose flour
- 2 teaspoons active dry yeast
- 1 pound bulk Italian sausage
- 1 can (26 ounces) garlic and herb spaghetti sauce, *divided*
- 3 tablespoons grated Parmesan cheese
- 1 jar (4-1/2 ounces) sliced mushrooms, drained
- 1/2 cup finely chopped green pepper
- 1/4 cup finely chopped onion
- 1-1/2 cups (6 ounces) shredded part-skim mozzarella cheese
- 1 egg, lightly beaten

1 In bread machine pan, place the first six ingredients in order suggested by manufacturer. Select dough setting (check dough after 5 minutes of mixing; add 1 to 2 tablespoons of water or flour if needed).

2 Meanwhile, in a large skillet, cook sausage over medium heat until no longer pink; drain and cool. When bread machine cycle is completed, turn dough onto a lightly floured surface. Roll out to a 15-in. circle. Transfer to a lightly greased baking sheet.

3 Spread 1/2 cup spaghetti sauce over half of circle to within 1/4 in. of edges. Layer with Parmesan cheese, sausage, mushrooms, green pepper, onion and mozzarella cheese. Fold dough over filling and pinch edges to seal.

4 With a sharp knife, make two slashes in dough; brush with egg. Bake at 350° for 40-45 minutes or until golden brown. Let stand for 5 minutes before cutting into six wedges. Warm remaining spaghetti sauce; serve with calzone.

garbanzo bean pitas

PREP/TOTAL TIME: 20 min. | **YIELD:** 4 servings.

This a wonderful meatless recipe for informal dinners and quick lunches. I add a little horseradish to my pitas for extra flair. SUSAN LE BRUN, SULPHUR, LOUISIANA

- 1 can (15 ounces) garbanzo beans *or* chickpeas, rinsed and drained
- 1/2 cup fat-free mayonnaise
- 1 tablespoon water
- 2 tablespoons minced fresh parsley
- 2 tablespoons chopped walnuts
- 1 tablespoon chopped onion
- 1 garlic clove, minced
- 1/8 teaspoon pepper
- 2 whole wheat pita pocket halves
- 4 lettuce leaves
- 1/2 small cucumber, thinly sliced
- 1 small tomato, seeded and chopped
- 1/4 cup fat-free ranch salad dressing, optional

1 In a blender, combine the first eight ingredients; cover and process until blended. Spoon 1/3 cup bean mixture into each pita half. Top with lettuce, cucumber and tomato. Serve with ranch dressing if desired.

hearty sirloin pitas

PREP/TOTAL TIME: 20 min. | **YIELD:** 4 servings.

Blue cheese takes the flavor of colorful sandwiches to the next level. To soften the pitas, warm them in the oven or microwave. TASTE OF HOME TEST KITCHEN

1-1/4	pounds beef top sirloin steak, cut into 1/4-inch slices
1/4	teaspoon salt
1/4	teaspoon pepper
3	teaspoons olive oil, *divided*
2-1/3	cups frozen pepper strips, thawed
1/2	cup thinly sliced onion
2	teaspoons A1 steak sauce
4	whole pita breads, warmed
1/4	cup crumbled blue cheese

1 Sprinkle beef with salt and pepper. In a large skillet, cook beef in batches in 2 teaspoons oil over medium heat until meat reaches desired doneness. Remove and keep warm.

2 In the same pan, saute pepper strips and onion in remaining oil until crisp-tender. Add beef and steak sauce; heat through.

3 Top each pita with the beef mixture; sprinkle with the cheese. Fold over.

mini greek burgers

PREP/TOTAL TIME: 30 min. | **YIELD:** 4 servings.

I substitute ground turkey for a less expensive version of lamb burgers. Serving it in a pita pocket is a fun and different twist on the regular burger in a bun.
NICHOLE HELMS, PIQUA, OHIO

3/4	cup shredded seeded peeled cucumber
1/2	cup plain yogurt
2	teaspoons lemon juice
2	teaspoons snipped fresh dill
1	garlic clove, minced
1/4	teaspoon salt
1/8	teaspoon pepper

MINI BURGERS:

3	tablespoons finely chopped onion
3	tablespoons minced fresh parsley
3/4	teaspoon dried oregano
1/4	teaspoon salt
1/4	teaspoon pepper
1	pound ground turkey
4	pita breads (6 inches), halved and warmed
2	medium tomatoes, thinly sliced

1 In a small bowl, combine the first seven ingredients. Cover and refrigerate until serving.

2 In a large bowl, combine the onion, parsley, oregano, salt and pepper. Crumble turkey over mixture and mix well. Shape into sixteen 2-in. patties.

3 Moisten a paper towel with cooking oil; using long-handled tongs, lightly coat the grill rack. Grill burgers, covered, over medium heat or broil 4 in. from the grill for 2-3 minutes on each side or until no longer pink. Serve in pita halves with tomatoes and reserved sauce.

reuben braids

PREP: 15 min. | **BAKE:** 25 min.
YIELD: 2 loaves (8 servings each).

I came up with this as a way to make a sandwich feed a large group at once. The braid design always impresses the guests at our parties. KELLIE MULLEAVY, LAMBERTVILLE, MICHIGAN

- 6 ounces cooked corned beef brisket, chopped (about 1 cup)
- 1-1/2 cups (6 ounces) shredded Swiss cheese
- 3/4 cup sauerkraut, rinsed and well drained
- 1 small onion, chopped
- 3 tablespoons Thousand Island salad dressing
- 1 tablespoon Dijon mustard
- 1/2 teaspoon dill weed
- 2 packages (8 ounces each) refrigerated crescent rolls
- 1 egg white, lightly beaten
- 1 tablespoon sesame seeds

1 In a large bowl, combine the first seven ingredients. Unroll one tube of crescent dough onto an ungreased baking sheet; seal seams and perforations.

2 Spread half of corned beef filling down center of rectangle. On each long side, cut 1-in.-wide strips to within 1 in. of filling. Starting at one end, fold alternating strips at an angle across filling; seal ends. Repeat with remaining crescent dough and filling. Brush egg white over braids; sprinkle with sesame seeds.

3 Bake at 375° for 25-30 minutes or until golden brown. Cool on wire racks for 5 minutes before cutting into slices. Refrigerate any leftovers.

tender chicken pockets

PREP/TOTAL TIME: 15 min. | **YIELD:** 2 servings.

Our weekend lunches had gotten bland and boring, so I concocted this flavorful recipe that's now a family favorite. Try it with a fruit salad on the side to round out the meal.
BETH WOODARD, JAMESTOWN, NORTH CAROLINA

- 1/2 pound boneless skinless chicken breasts, cubed
- 1 cup water
- 1 teaspoon beef bouillon granules
- 4 teaspoons Dijon mustard
- 4 teaspoons mayonnaise, optional
- 4 whole wheat pita pocket halves
- 4 lettuce leaves
- 1/2 cup sliced cucumber
- 1/2 cup shredded cheddar cheese

Dash salt and pepper

1 In a microwave-safe bowl, combine the chicken, water and bouillon. Cover and microwave on high for 3-4 minutes or until meat is no longer pink.

2 Spread mustard and mayonnaise if desired on the inside of each pita half. Fill with lettuce, cucumber, chicken and cheese. Season with salt and pepper.

EDITOR'S NOTE: This recipe was tested in a 1,100-watt microwave.

tip A dash is a very small amount of seasoning added with a quick downward stroke of the hand. A pinch, on the other hand, is the amount of a dry ingredient that can be held between your thumb and forefinger.

pepper pork pockets

PREP/TOTAL TIME: 25 min. | **YIELD:** 3 servings.

I pair these pork pita pockets with traditional pasta salad and a medley of sliced tomatoes, carrots and cucumbers. If you're a time-pressed cook like me, save time by making the garlic sauce up to two days in advance and storing it in the refrigerator until ready to serve.

PAULA MARCHESI, LENHARTSVILLE, PENNSYLVANIA

- 1 pound boneless pork loin chops, cut into thin 2-inch strips
- 1 teaspoon pepper
- 1/2 teaspoon salt
- 1 tablespoon olive oil
- 1 jar (7 ounces) roasted sweet red peppers, drained and coarsely chopped
- 1/2 cup mayonnaise
- 2 tablespoons milk
- 1 teaspoon minced garlic
- 6 lettuce leaves
- 3 pita breads (6 inches), halved and warmed

1 Sprinkle pork with pepper and salt. In a large skillet, saute pork in oil until juices run clear. Add red peppers; cook and stir until heated through. Remove from the heat.

2 In a large bowl, combine the mayonnaise, milk and garlic. Spoon pork mixture into lettuce-lined pita halves. Drizzle with the dressing.

beefy swiss bundles

PREP: 20 min. | **BAKE:** 20 min. | **YIELD:** 4 servings.

Kids and adults alike will devour these comforting beef bundles. With creamy mashed potatoes, gooey cheese and a host of flavorful seasonings, what's not to love?

TASTE OF HOME TEST KITCHEN

- 1 pound ground beef
- 1-1/2 cups sliced fresh mushrooms
- 1/2 cup chopped onion
- 1-1/2 teaspoons minced garlic
- 4 teaspoons Worcestershire sauce
- 3/4 teaspoon dried rosemary, crushed
- 3/4 teaspoon paprika
- 1/2 teaspoon salt
- 1/4 teaspoon pepper
- 1 sheet frozen puff pastry, thawed
- 2/3 cup refrigerated mashed potatoes
- 1 cup (4 ounces) shredded Swiss cheese
- 1 egg
- 2 tablespoons water

1 In a large skillet, cook the beef, mushrooms and onion over medium heat until meat is no longer pink. Add garlic; cook 1 minute longer. Drain. Stir in Worcestershire sauce and seasonings. Remove from the heat; set aside.

2 On a lightly floured surface, roll puff pastry into a 15-in. x 13-in. rectangle. Cut into four 7-1/2-in. x 6-1/2-in. rectangles. Place about 2 tablespoons potatoes over each rectangle; spread to within 1 in. of edges. Top with 3/4 cup beef mixture; sprinkle with 1/4 cup cheese.

3 Beat the egg and water; brush some over pastry edges. Bring opposite corners of pastry over each bundle; pinch seams to seal. Transfer to a greased baking sheet; brush with remaining egg mixture. Bake at 400° for 17-20 minutes or until golden brown.

artichoke chicken pockets

PREP: 20 min. | **BAKE:** 15 min. | **YIELD:** 6 servings.

You'll have a hard time believing these hefty, pizza-crust pockets are light! Packed full of cheese, artichokes, chicken and spinach, they make a filling and nutritious lunch. They even taste fantastic without the marinara sauce.

BEVERLY O'FERRALL, LINKWOOD, MARYLAND

- 2 cups shredded cooked chicken breast
- 2 cups thinly sliced fresh spinach
- 1-1/4 cups shredded provolone cheese
- 3/4 cup water-packed artichoke hearts, rinsed, drained and chopped
- 1 garlic clove, minced
- 1/4 teaspoon pepper
- 1 tube (13.8 ounces) refrigerated pizza crust
- 2 teaspoons cornmeal

Marinara sauce, optional

1 In a large bowl, combine the first six ingredients. Unroll pizza dough; cut into six 4-1/2-in. squares. Spoon 1 cup chicken mixture onto the center of each square; brush edges of dough with water. Fold one corner of each square over filling to the opposite corner, forming a triangle. Using a fork, crimp edges to seal.

2 Sprinkle cornmeal over a 15-in. x 10-in. x 1-in. baking pan coated with cooking spray. Place pockets in pan; prick tops with a fork. Bake at 425° for 12-15 minutes or until golden brown. Serve with marinara sauce if desired.

french cheeseburger loaf

PREP: 25 min. | **BAKE:** 25 min. | **YIELD:** 6 servings.

Once you prepare this impressive, yet simple-to-make sandwich, you'll never look at refrigerated bread dough the same. It's one of the easiest recipes I have in my files.

NANCY DAUGHERTY, CORTLAND, OHIO

- 3/4 pound lean ground beef (90% lean)
- 1/2 cup chopped sweet onion
- 1 small green pepper, chopped
- 2 garlic cloves, minced
- 2 tablespoons all-purpose flour
- 2 tablespoons Dijon mustard
- 1 tablespoon ketchup
- 1 tube (11 ounces) refrigerated crusty French loaf
- 4 slices reduced-fat process American cheese product
- 1 egg white, lightly beaten
- 3 tablespoons shredded Parmesan cheese

1 In a large skillet, cook the beef, onion and pepper over medium heat until meat is no longer pink. Add garlic; cook 1 minute longer. Stir in the flour, mustard and ketchup; set aside.

2 Unroll dough starting at the seam. Pat into a 14-in. x 12-in. rectangle. Spoon meat mixture lengthwise down the center of the dough; top with cheese slices. Bring long sides of dough to the center over filling; pinch seams to seal.

3 Place seam side down on a baking sheet coated with cooking spray. Brush with egg white. Sprinkle with Parmesan cheese.

4 With a sharp knife, cut diagonal slits in top of loaf. Bake at 350° for 25-30 minutes or until golden brown. Serve warm.

pepper steak quesadillas

PREP/TOTAL TIME: 30 min. | **YIELD:** 4 servings.

I came up with these savory quesadillas when my family needed a quick meal before running off in several directions. I threw together what I had in the fridge, and it was a big hit! BARBARA MOORE, FARMINGTON, NEW MEXICO

- 1/2   pound beef top sirloin steak
- 1/2   *each* medium green, sweet red and yellow pepper, julienned
- 1   tablespoon chopped red onion
- 1   garlic clove, minced
- 1   tablespoon minced fresh cilantro
- 1/4   teaspoon dried rosemary, crushed
- 4   flour tortillas (6 inches)
- 6   cherry tomatoes, halved
- 1/4   cup sliced fresh mushrooms
- 1   cup (4 ounces) shredded part-skim mozzarella cheese

1 Moisten a paper towel with cooking oil; using long-handled tongs, lightly coat the grill rack. Grill steak, covered, over medium heat or broil 4 in. from the heat for 4 minutes on each side or until meat reaches desired doneness (for medium-rare, a meat thermometer should read 145°; medium, 160°; well-done, 170°). Let stand for 10 minutes.

2 Meanwhile, in a large skillet coated with cooking spray, saute peppers and onion for 5-6 minutes or until tender. Add garlic; cook 1 minute longer. Sprinkle with cilantro and rosemary.

3 Place two tortillas on a baking sheet coated with cooking spray. Cut steak into thin strips; place on tortillas. Using a slotted spoon, place pepper mixture over steak. Top with tomatoes, mushrooms, cheese and remaining tortillas; lightly spray top of tortillas with cooking spray.

4 Bake at 425° for 5-10 minutes or until golden brown and cheese is melted. Cut each quesadilla into four wedges.

sausage sandwich squares

PREP: 35 min. + rising | **BAKE:** 20 min. | **YIELD:** 12-15 servings.

My husband and I teach Sunday school and lead youth groups at our church, so I needed a tasty recipe to feed a group of hungry teens. They loved this pizza-like sandwich.
MARY MERRILL, BLOOMINGDALE, OHIO

- 1 package (1/4 ounce) active dry yeast
- 1-1/3 cups warm water (110° to 115°), *divided*
- 1/2 teaspoon salt
- 3 to 3-1/2 cups all-purpose flour
- 1 pound bulk Italian sausage
- 1 medium sweet red pepper, diced
- 1 medium green pepper, diced
- 1 large onion, diced
- 4 cups (16 ounces) shredded part-skim mozzarella cheese
- 1 egg
- 1 tablespoon water
- 2 tablespoons grated Parmesan cheese
- 2 tablespoons minced fresh parsley
- 1/2 teaspoon dried oregano
- 1/8 teaspoon garlic powder

1 In a large bowl, dissolve yeast in 1/2 cup warm water. Add the salt, remaining water and 2 cups flour. Beat until smooth. Add enough remaining flour to form a firm dough.

2 Turn onto a floured surface; knead until smooth and elastic, about 6 minutes. Place in a greased bowl, turning once to grease top. Cover and let rise in a warm place until doubled, about 50 minutes.

3 In a large skillet, cook sausage over medium heat until no longer pink; remove with a slotted spoon and set aside. In the drippings, saute peppers and onion until tender; drain.

4 Press half of the dough onto the bottom and 1/2 in. up the sides of a greased 15-in. x 10-in. x 1-in. baking pan. Spread sausage evenly over the crust. Top with peppers and onion. Sprinkle with mozzarella cheese. Roll out remaining dough to fit pan; place over cheese and seal the edges.

5 In a small bowl, beat egg and water. Stir in the remaining ingredients. Brush over dough. Cut slits in top. Bake at 400° for 20-25 minutes or until golden brown. Cut into squares.

fried chicken pitas

PREP/TOTAL TIME: 10 min. | **YIELD:** 6 servings.

These pitas are a fun twist on classic fried chicken. They make great picnic fare. JENNIFER VENEZIANO, CARMEL, INDIANA

- 3 cups thinly sliced fried chicken (including crispy skin)
- 1 cup coleslaw salad dressing
- 1/3 cup crumbled cooked bacon
- 2 tablespoons chopped green onions with tops
- 1/4 teaspoon ground mustard
- 1/8 teaspoon pepper
- 6 pita bread halves

1 In a large bowl, combine the chicken, dressing, bacon, onions, mustard and pepper. Spoon into pita bread.

greek salad pitas

PREP/TOTAL TIME: 20 min. | **YIELD:** 2 servings.

Veggie lovers rejoice! This meatless pita is stuffed with plenty of chopped vegetables and savory Greek accents. It's so hearty and delicious that no one will even miss the meat!

ALEXIS WORCHESKY-LASEK, WEST FRIENDSHIP, MARYLAND

- 2/3 cup chopped seeded cucumber
- 2/3 cup chopped sweet red pepper
- 2/3 cup chopped tomato
- 2/3 cup chopped zucchini
- 1/4 cup crumbled feta cheese
- 2 tablespoons chopped ripe olives
- 2 teaspoons red wine vinegar
- 2 teaspoons lemon juice
- 3/4 teaspoon dried oregano
- 1/8 teaspoon salt
- 1/8 teaspoon pepper
- 4 lettuce leaves
- 2 pita breads (6 inches), halved

1 In a small bowl, combine the cucumber, red pepper, tomato, zucchini, feta cheese and olives. In another bowl, whisk the vinegar, lemon juice, oregano, salt and pepper. Pour the dressing over the vegetables and toss to coat. Spoon the mixture into lettuce-lined pita halves.

fruity peanut butter pitas

PREP/TOTAL TIME: 5 min. | **YIELD:** 2 servings.

My kids love these fruit-filled delights. You can also skip the pita bread and cut a cored apple into horizontal slices. Spread the spiced peanut butter with tiny banana chunks in between two apple slices for a fun mini sandwich.

KIM HOLMES, EMERALD PARK, SASKATCHEWAN

- 1/4 cup peanut butter
- 1/8 teaspoon *each* ground allspice, cinnamon and nutmeg
- 2 whole wheat pita pocket halves
- 1/2 medium apple, thinly sliced
- 1/2 medium firm banana, sliced

1 In a bowl, blend the peanut butter and spices. Spread inside pita bread halves; fill with apple and banana slices.

tip Here are some handy banana basics. Look for plump bananas that are evenly yellow-colored. Green bananas are under-ripe, while a flecking of brown flecks indicates ripeness. If bananas are too green, place in a paper bag until ripe. Adding an apple to the bag will speed the process. Store ripe bananas at room temperature. To prevent bruises, a banana hook or hanger is a great inexpensive investment. For longer storage, you can place ripe bananas in a tightly sealed plastic bag and refrigerate. The peel will become brown but the flesh will remain unchanged. One pound of bananas equals about 3 medium or 1-1/3 cups mashed.

EASY CHERRY STRUDELS, PG. 102

dessert sandwiches

WHOOPIE PIES, PG. 106

ICE CREAM TACOS, PG. 106

chocolate crepes
with raspberry sauce

PREP: 25 min. + chilling | **COOK:** 20 min. | **YIELD:** 8 servings.

Here is a scrumptious treat everyone at the table can enjoy without guilt. Seemingly rich and decadent, each crepe has only 2 grams of fat per serving! How sweet is that?
REBECCA BAIRD, SALT LAKE CITY, UTAH

  1 **cup fat-free milk**
1/2 **cup fat-free evaporated milk**
  2 **egg whites**
  1 **egg**
  1 **cup all-purpose flour**
1/4 **cup plus 1/3 cup sugar,** *divided*
1/4 **cup baking cocoa**
1/2 **teaspoon salt**
4-1/2 **teaspoons cornstarch**
  1 **cup water**
4-1/2 **cups fresh** *or* **frozen raspberries, thawed,** *divided*
Reduced-fat whipped cream in a can
  1 **teaspoon confectioners' sugar**

1 In a small bowl, combine the milk, evaporated milk, egg whites and egg. Combine the flour, 1/4 cup sugar, cocoa and salt; add to milk mixture and mix well. Cover and refrigerate for 1 hour.

2 In a small saucepan, combine cornstarch and remaining sugar; set aside. Place water and 3-1/2 cups raspberries in a blender; cover and process for 2-3 minutes or until pureed.

3 Strain puree into cornstarch mixture and discard seeds. Bring to a boil; cook and stir for 2 minutes or until thickened. Transfer to a small bowl; refrigerate until chilled.

4 Coat an 8-in. nonstick skillet with cooking spray; heat over medium heat. Stir crepe batter; pour a scant 3 tablespoons into center of skillet. Lift and tilt pan to coat bottom evenly. Cook until top appears dry; turn and cook 15-20 seconds longer. Remove to a wire rack.

5 Repeat with remaining batter, coating skillet with cooking spray as needed. When cool, stack crepes with waxed paper or paper towels in between.

6 Spread each crepe with 2 tablespoons sauce. Fold each crepe into quarters; place two crepes on each of eight individual plates. Top servings with remaining sauce and 1 tablespoon whipped cream. Garnish with remaining raspberries and sprinkle with confectioners' sugar.

golden apple bundles

PREP: 20 min. | **BAKE:** 25 min. | **YIELD:** 10-12 servings.

This recipe is a delightful way to make use of apples. I often whip up these hand-held bundles on Fridays, so I have a dessert ready to serve on the weekend. They bake up flaky and golden brown on the outside and moist and tender on the inside. LILA ELLER, EVERETT, WASHINGTON

  2 **cups chopped peeled apples**
1/3 **cup chopped walnuts**
1/4 **cup packed brown sugar**
1/4 **cup raisins**
  1 **tablespoon all-purpose flour**
1/2 **teaspoon lemon peel**
1/2 **teaspoon ground cinnamon**
Pastry for double-crust pie
Milk
Sugar

1 In a large bowl, combine the apples, walnuts, brown sugar, raisins, flour, lemon peel and cinnamon; set aside.

2 Roll pastry to 1/8-in. thickness. Cut into 5-in. circles. Spoon about 1/4 cup apple mixture into center of each circle. Moisten edges of pastry with water. Fold over and seal edges with a fork.

3 Place on a greased baking sheet. Bake at 450° for 10 minutes. Reduce heat to 400° bake 10 minutes longer. Brush each with milk and sprinkle with sugar; return to oven for 5 minutes.

easy cherry strudels

PREP: 15 min. | **BAKE:** 20 min. | **YIELD:** 2 strudels (5 slices each).

The original recipe for these strudels called for phyllo dough. One day I bought puff pastry by mistake, but was pleased to discover it cut down significantly on prep time.

SUSAN DANCY, TALLAHASSEE, FLORIDA

1	can (14-1/2 ounces) pitted tart cherries
1	cup sugar
1/2	cup dried cranberries *or* raisins
1	tablespoon butter
3	tablespoons cornstarch
1-1/2	cups chopped walnuts
1	package (17.3 ounces) frozen puff pastry, thawed
1	egg, lightly beaten

1 Drain cherries, reserving 1/3 cup juice. In a large saucepan, combine the cherries, sugar, cranberries and butter. Cook and stir over medium heat until heated through. Combine cornstarch and reserved juice and add to the pan. Bring to a boil. Cook and stir 1-2 minutes longer or until thickened. Remove from the heat; stir in walnuts.

2 Unfold one pastry sheet and cut in half. Mound half of the cherry mixture on one pastry half to within 1/2 in. of edges. Top with remaining pastry half; pinch edges to seal. Repeat with remaining pastry and filling.

3 Place on a greased foil-lined baking sheet. With a sharp knife, cut diagonal slits into tops of strudels; brush with egg. Bake at 400° for 20-25 minutes or until golden brown.

peanut butter ice cream sandwiches

PREP: 45 min. | **BAKE:** 10 min. + freezing | **YIELD:** 16 servings.

This frozen dessert takes the classic peanut butter cookie up a notch by adding in dark chocolate and vanilla ice cream.

TERESA GAETZKE, NORTH FREEDOM, WISCONSIN

1/2	cup shortening
1/2	cup creamy peanut butter
3/4	cup sugar, *divided*
1/2	cup packed brown sugar
1	egg
1/2	teaspoon vanilla extract
1-1/2	cups all-purpose flour
1	teaspoon baking soda
1/2	teaspoon salt
12	ounces dark chocolate candy coating, chopped
1	quart vanilla ice cream, softened

1 In a large bowl, cream the shortening, peanut butter, 1/2 cup sugar and brown sugar until light and fluffy. Beat in egg and vanilla. Combine the flour, baking soda and salt; gradually add to creamed mixture and mix well.

2 Roll dough into 1-in. balls; roll in remaining sugar. Place 1 in. apart on ungreased baking sheets. Flatten with a fork, forming a crisscross pattern.

3 Bake at 350° for 9-11 minutes or until set (do not overbake). Remove to wire racks to cool completely.

4 In a microwave, melt candy coating; stir until smooth. Spread a heaping teaspoonful on the bottom of each cookie; place chocolate side up on waxed paper until set.

5 To make sandwiches, place 1/4 cup ice cream on the bottom of half of the cookies; top with remaining cookies. Wrap in plastic wrap; freeze.

cherry-chocolate cream puffs

PREP: 30 min. + cooling | **BAKE:** 30 min. + cooling
YIELD: 10 servings.

Celebrate cream puffs in all their lusciousness with this version featuring the sweet flavors of cherry and chocolate.
CHRISTOPHER FUSON, MARYSVILLE, OHIO

- 1 cup water
- 1/3 cup butter, cubed
- 1 tablespoon sugar
- 1/8 teaspoon salt
- 1 cup all-purpose flour
- 4 eggs

CHERRY-CHOCOLATE FILLING:

- 1 carton (8 ounces) frozen whipped topping, thawed
- 1/2 cup sugar
- 1/4 cup 2% milk
- 6 ounces semisweet chocolate, chopped
- 3/4 pound fresh *or* frozen sweet cherries, thawed, pitted and chopped

Confectioners' sugar

1 In a small saucepan over medium heat, bring the water, butter, sugar and salt to a boil. Add flour all at once; stir until a smooth ball forms. Remove from the heat; let stand for 5 minutes. Add eggs, one at a time, beating well after each addition. Continue beating until mixture is smooth and shiny.

2 Drop by 2 rounded tablespoonfuls 3 in. apart onto greased baking sheets. Bake at 400° for 30-35 minutes or until golden brown. Remove to wire racks. Immediately split puffs open; remove tops and set aside. Discard soft dough from inside. Cool puffs.

3 Let whipped topping stand at room temperature for 30 minutes. Meanwhile, in a small saucepan over medium heat, bring sugar and milk to a boil; cook and stir until sugar is dissolved. Reduce heat to low; stir in chocolate until melted.

4 Transfer to a large bowl. Cool to room temperature, about 25 minutes, stirring occasionally. Fold in whipped topping.

5 Fill each cream puff with a heaping tablespoonful of cherries; top with chocolate filling. Replace tops. Dust with confectioners' sugar; serve immediately. Refrigerate leftovers.

strawberry cheese bundles

PREP/TOTAL TIME: 25 min. | **YIELD:** 8 servings.

These heavenly little sandwiches taste like something you'd purchase from a bakery. Folks are always surprised to learn they start with convenient refrigerated crescent rolls and pie filling. JOLENE SPRAY, VAN WERT, OHIO

- 1 package (3 ounces) cream cheese, softened
- 2 tablespoons confectioners' sugar
- 1/4 teaspoon almond extract
- 1 tube (8 ounces) refrigerated crescent rolls
- 1/3 cup strawberry pie filling
- 1/3 cup crushed pineapple, drained
- 2 to 3 tablespoons apricot spreadable fruit

1 In a small bowl, beat the cream cheese, sugar and extract until smooth. Unroll crescent dough and separate into eight triangles. Place 1 heaping teaspoonful of cream cheese mixture in the center of each triangle. Top with 1 teaspoon of pie filling and 1 teaspoon of pineapple.

2 With one long side of pastry facing you, fold right and left corners over filling to top corner, forming a square. Seal edges. Place on an ungreased baking sheet. Bake at 375° for 15-17 minutes or until lightly browned. Brush with spreadable fruit. Serve warm or cold.

chocolate mint sandwich cookies

PREP: 20 min. | **BAKE:** 10 min./batch + cooling
YIELD: about 2-1/2 dozen sandwich cookies.

Mint lovers rejoice! These cookie-jar delights are too good to stop at just one. BERTHA BRATT, LYNDEN, WASHINGTON

- 6 tablespoons butter, cubed
- 1-1/2 cups packed brown sugar
- 2 tablespoons water
- 2 cups (12 ounces) semisweet chocolate chips
- 2 eggs
- 1 teaspoon vanilla extract
- 2-1/2 cups all-purpose flour
- 1-1/2 teaspoons baking soda
- 1 teaspoon salt

FILLING:
- 2-1/2 cups confectioners' sugar
- 1/4 cup butter, softened
- 3 tablespoons milk
- 1/2 teaspoon peppermint extract
- 3 drops green food coloring, optional

Dash salt

1 In a small saucepan, combine the butter, brown sugar, water and chocolate chips. Cook and stir over low heat until chips are melted. Cool. Beat in eggs and vanilla. Combine the flour, baking soda and salt; gradually add to chocolate mixture.

2 Drop by rounded teaspoonfuls 2 in. apart onto ungreased baking sheets. Bake at 350° for 10-12 minutes or until firm. Remove to wire racks to cool.

3 In a large bowl, combine filling ingredients until smooth. Spread on the bottoms of half the cookies; top with remaining cookies.

cherry-chip ice cream sandwiches

PREP: 15 min. + chilling | **PROCESS:** 20 min. + freezing
YIELD: 10 servings.

These marvelous ice cream treats are a great way to cool down on a hot summer day. Make them in advance and store in the freezer. SALLY HOOK, MONTGOMERY, TEXAS

- 1-1/2 cups 2% milk
- 1/2 cup sugar

Dash salt
- 1 cup heavy whipping cream
- 1 teaspoon vanilla extract
- 2/3 cup chopped dried cherries
- 1/2 cup miniature semisweet chocolate chips
- 10 whole chocolate graham crackers

1 In a large saucepan over medium heat, cook and stir the milk, sugar and salt until sugar is dissolved. Remove from the heat; stir in cream and vanilla. Transfer to a bowl; refrigerate until chilled.

2 Line a 13-in. x 9-in. pan with waxed paper; set aside. Fill cylinder of ice cream freezer with milk mixture; freeze according to manufacturer's directions. Stir in cherries and chocolate chips. Spread into prepared pan; cover and freeze overnight.

3 Cut or break graham crackers in half. Using waxed paper, lift ice cream out of pan; discard waxed paper. Cut ice cream into squares the same size as the graham cracker halves; place ice cream between cracker halves. Wrap sandwiches in plastic wrap. Freeze until serving.

chocolate-almond dessert crepes

PREP: 15 min. + chilling | **COOK:** 25 min. | **YIELD:** 12 servings.

Who can resist a tender crepe filled with a rich, homemade chocolate filling and sprinkled with crunchy almonds? It's one sensation that will make a sweet finale to any special-occasion meal. TASTE OF HOME COOKING SCHOOL

1-1/4 cups milk
   3 eggs
   2 tablespoons butter, melted
3/4 cup all-purpose flour
   1 tablespoon sugar
1/4 teaspoon salt
   1 envelope unflavored gelatin
   2 tablespoons cold water
1/4 cup boiling water
   1 cup sugar
1/2 cup baking cocoa
   2 cups cold heavy whipping cream
   2 teaspoons vanilla extract
Chocolate fudge ice cream topping and whipped topping
1/2 cup sliced almonds, toasted

1 In a large bowl, combine the milk, eggs and butter. Combine the flour, sugar and salt; add to milk mixture and beat until smooth. Cover and refrigerate for 1 hour.

2 Meanwhile, in a small bowl, sprinkle gelatin over cold water; let stand for 2 minutes to soften. Add boiling water; stir until gelatin is completely dissolved and mixture is clear. Cool slightly.

3 In a large bowl, mix the sugar and cocoa; add cream and vanilla. Beat on medium speed until well blended. Cover and refrigerate at least 30 minutes.

4 Heat a lightly greased 8-in. nonstick skillet. Stir batter; pour 1/4 cup batter into the center of skillet. Lift and tilt pan to evenly coat bottom. Cook until top appears dry; turn and cook 15-20 seconds longer. Remove to a wire rack. Repeat with remaining batter, greasing skillet as needed. Stack crepes with waxed paper or paper towels in between.

5 Spoon or pipe chocolate filling down the center of each crepe; roll up. Drizzle with fudge topping and garnish with whipped topping. Sprinkle with almonds.

whoopie pies

PREP: 15 min. | **BAKE:** 5 min./batch + cooling | **YIELD:** 1-1/2 dozen.

My famous whoopie pies feature an irresistible cream filling sandwiched between two chocolate cupcake-like cookies. Enlist the kids to help assemble these old-fashioned favorites. RUTH ANN STELFOX, RAYMOND, ALBERTA

- 1 cup butter, softened
- 1-1/2 cups sugar
- 2 eggs
- 2 teaspoons vanilla extract
- 4 cups all-purpose flour
- 3/4 cup baking cocoa
- 2 teaspoons baking soda
- 1/2 teaspoon salt
- 1 cup water
- 1 cup buttermilk

FILLING:

- 2 cups confectioners' sugar
- 2 cups marshmallow creme
- 1/2 cup butter, softened
- 2 teaspoons vanilla extract

1 In a large bowl, cream butter and sugar until light and fluffy. Beat in eggs and vanilla. Combine the flour, cocoa, baking soda and salt; add to creamed mixture alternately with water and buttermilk, beating well after each addition.

2 Drop by tablespoonfuls 2 in. apart onto greased baking sheets. Bake at 375° for 5-7 minutes or until set. Remove to wire racks to cool completely.

3 In a small bowl, beat filling ingredients until fluffy. Spread on the bottoms of half of the cookies; top with remaining cookies.

ice cream tacos

PREP: 30 min. | **BAKE:** 10 min./batch + cooling | **YIELD:** 16 tacos.

These ice cream-filled sandwiches are fun to make and even more fun to eat. They're great party treats, and folks young and old will have a ball putting them together.

NANCY ZIMMERMAN, CAPE MAY COURT HOUSE, NEW JERSEY

- 1/2 cup packed brown sugar
- 1/3 cup butter, melted
- 1/4 cup honey
- 3/4 cup all-purpose flour
- 1/2 teaspoon water
- 4 to 5 drops green food coloring
- 1 cup flaked coconut
- 1/2 gallon chocolate ice cream
- 1 cup whipped topping

Red, orange and yellow M&M's milk chocolate miniature baking bits

1 Using a pencil, draw two 3-in. circles on a sheet of parchment paper. Place paper, pencil mark side down, on a baking sheet; set aside.

2 In a large bowl, beat the brown sugar, butter and honey until blended. Add flour; mix well (batter will be thick). Spread 1 tablespoon of batter over each circle.

3 Bake at 350° for 6-7 minutes or until golden brown. Cool for 2 minutes. Loosen each cookie and curl around a rolling pin to form a taco shell. Cool completely before removing to a wire rack. Repeat with remaining batter.

4 In a small resealable plastic bag, combine the water and food coloring; add coconut. Seal the bag and shake to tint. Fill the taco shells with ice cream; garnish with the whipped topping, coconut and M&M's.

hazelnut apricot strudel

PREP: 30 min. + cooling | **BAKE:** 15 min. + cooling
YIELD: 8 servings.

Did you know "strudel" is the German word for whirlpool? The swirled layers of this rolled dessert likely led to its unique name. But no matter what you call it, it's guaranteed to please! TASTE OF HOME TEST KITCHEN

1	package (6 ounces) dried apricots, chopped
1/4	cup sugar
1	teaspoon orange peel
1/2	cup orange juice
1/4	cup water
1/3	cup chopped hazelnuts
6	sheets phyllo dough (14 inches x 9 inches)
2	tablespoons butter, melted
1/3	cup graham cracker crumbs (about 5 squares)

1 In a small saucepan, combine the apricots, sugar and peel. Stir in orange juice and water. Bring to a boil. Reduce heat; simmer, uncovered, for 15 minutes or until juice is absorbed, stirring occasionally. Remove from the heat and cool to room temperature. Set aside 1 tablespoon nuts; toast the remaining nuts. Stir into the apricot mixture.

2 Place one sheet of phyllo dough on a work surface; brush with butter and sprinkle with 1 tablespoon of crumbs. Repeat with 5 more sheets of phyllo; brushing each layer with butter and sprinkling with crumbs. (Keep remaining phyllo covered with plastic wrap and a damp towel to prevent it from drying out.)

3 Carefully spread filling along one long edge to within 2 in. of edges. Fold the two short sides over filling. Roll up jelly-roll style, starting with a long side.

4 Place seam side down on a greased baking sheet. Brush the top with butter and score top lightly every 1-1/2 in. Sprinkle with the reserved nuts.

5 Bake at 375° for 15 minutes or until golden brown. Cool on a wire rack. Slice at scored marks.

black forest crepes

PREP/TOTAL TIME: 20 min. | **YIELD:** 8 servings.

Cherries and chocolate are a match made in heaven, but the combination is even better when enhanced by tender crepes and a luscious cream cheese filling.
MARY RELYEA, CANASTOTA, NEW YORK

1	package (8 ounces) reduced-fat cream cheese, softened
1/2	cup reduced-fat sour cream
1/2	teaspoon vanilla extract
2/3	cup confectioners' sugar
8	prepared crepes (9 inches)
1	can (20 ounces) reduced-sugar cherry pie filling, warmed
1/4	cup chocolate syrup

1 In a small bowl, beat the cream cheese, sour cream and vanilla until smooth. Gradually beat in confectioners' sugar. Spread about 3 tablespoons over each crepe to within 1/2 in. of edges; roll up.

2 Arrange in an ungreased 13-in. x 9-in. baking dish. Bake, uncovered, at 350° for 5-7 minutes or until warm. To serve, top each crepe with 1/4 cup pie filling and drizzle with 1-1/2 teaspoons chocolate syrup.

tip Phyllo (pronounced FEE-lo) is a tissue-thin dough generally sold in the freezer section of grocery stores. Phyllo dough is liberally basted with melted butter between each sheet so that it bakes up crisp and flaky. Phyllo dough is used for desserts, appetizers and savory main dishes.

general category index

This index lists every sandwich by food category and/or major ingredient, so you can easily locate recipes that fit your needs.

singapore satay sandwiches, 26
tender chicken pockets, 94

CHOCOLATE
cherry-chip ice cream sandwiches, 104
cherry-chocolate cream puffs, 103
chocolate-almond dessert crepes, 105
chocolate crepes with raspberry sauce, 101
chocolate french toast, 13
chocolate mint sandwich cookies, 104
chocolate peanut butter sandwiches, 46
ice cream tacos, 106
peanut butter ice cream sandwiches, 102

COLD SANDWICHES
apple-swiss turkey sandwiches, 52
artichoke-lamb sandwich loaves, 58
beef sandwiches with beet spread, 47
bistro turkey sandwiches, 51
blts with raisin-avocado spread, 53
blue cheese clubs, 54
brickyard bistro sandwich, 56
cashew turkey salad sandwiches, 54
cherry-chicken salad croissants, 56
chicken salad sandwiches, 49
chickpea sandwich spread, 48
chocolate peanut butter sandwiches, 46
country ham sandwiches, 57
crab salad tea sandwiches, 10
creamy beef sandwiches, 53
cucumber sandwiches, 45
curried beef sandwiches, 44
fresh mozzarella sandwiches, 50
ham and swiss bagels, 51
ham salad croissants, 44
havarti turkey hero, 49
hearty veggie sandwiches, 59
lemony shrimp sandwiches, 45
lime-cilantro turkey hoagies, 55
mini chicken salad croissants, 10
mini muffuletta, 7
mini subs, 11
mom's egg salad sandwiches, 55
nutty marmalade sandwiches, 44
pbj on a stick, 11
pumpernickel turkey hero, 48
sandwich for 12, 46
savory sandwich ring, 57
simon's famous tuna salad, 45
spinach feta croissants for 2, 48
sunny blt sandwiches, 43
super-duper tuna sandwiches, 50
turkey focaccia club, 43
turkey salad sandwiches, 58
walnut-cream cheese finger sandwiches, 6

CUCUMBERS
apple-swiss turkey sandwiches, 52
artichoke-lamb sandwich loaves, 58
asian chicken salad, 64
beef gyros, 81
chicken tortillas, 78
crab salad pockets, 83
cucumber sandwiches, 45

garbanzo bean pitas, 92
greek salad pitas, 99
mini greek burgers, 93
pastrami deli wraps, 76
singapore satay sandwiches, 26
tender chicken pockets, 94

DESSERTS
black forest crepes, 107
caramel cream crepes, 20
cherry-chip ice cream sandwiches, 104
cherry-chocolate cream puffs, 103
chocolate-almond dessert crepes, 105
chocolate crepes with raspberry sauce, 101
chocolate mint sandwich cookies, 104
chocolate peanut butter sandwiches, 46
easy cherry strudels, 102
golden apple bundles, 101
hazelnut apricot strudel, 107
ice cream tacos, 106
peanut butter ice cream sandwiches, 102
strawberry cheese bundles, 103
whoopie pies, 106

EGGS
bistro breakfast panini, 16
breakfast biscuits 'n' eggs, 15
breakfast quesadillas, 20
crab salad tea sandwiches, 10
dad's quick bagel omelet sandwich, 14
egg salad english muffins, 13
egg salad roll-ups, 72
grandma's french tuna salad wraps, 63
ham & cheese breakfast strudels, 19
ham 'n' egg breakfast wraps, 21
ham pinwheels, 8
mom's egg salad sandwiches, 55
prosciutto egg panini, 18
scrambled egg wraps, 13
spanish-style brunch wraps, 18
star sandwiches, 8
sunny blt sandwiches, 43

FISH & SEAFOOD
crab salad pockets, 83
crab salad tea sandwiches, 10
grandma's french tuna salad wraps, 63
lemony shrimp sandwiches, 45
mango shrimp pitas, 91
open-faced tuna melts, 37
puffy lobster turnovers, 6
sailor sandwiches with caesar mayo, 27
seafood salad pitas, 89
simon's famous tuna salad, 45
smoked salmon appetizer crepes, 9
super-duper tuna sandwiches, 50
weeknight catfish wraps, 78

FRUIT
apple-swiss turkey sandwiches, 52
berry cream pancakes, 15
bistro turkey sandwiches, 51
blts with raisin-avocado spread, 53
cashew turkey salad sandwiches, 54

cherry-chicken salad croissants, 56
cherry-chip ice cream sandwiches, 104
cherry-chocolate cream puffs, 103
chicken salad sandwiches, 49
chocolate crepes with raspberry sauce, 101
easy cherry strudels, 102
fruit-filled french toast wraps, 17
fruited turkey salad pitas, 83
fruity peanut butter pitas, 99
golden apple bundles, 101
gourmet deli turkey wraps, 69
ham & apple grilled cheese sandwiches, 25
ham and apricot crepes, 17
ham and mango wraps, 76
hazelnut apricot strudel, 107
lemony shrimp sandwiches, 45
lime-cilantro turkey hoagies, 55
lime jalapeno turkey wraps, 65
pear waldorf pitas, 84
pork tenderloin panini with fig port jam, 41

GROUND BEEF
(ALSO SEE BEEF & CORNED BEEF)
aloha burgers, 28
basil burgers, 23
beef-stuffed crescents, 9
beefy swiss bundles, 95
burritos made easy, 65
cajun burgers, 30
cheeseburger pockets, 87
coney dogs, 28
flatbread tacos with ranch sour cream, 84
french cheeseburger loaf, 96
italian patty melts, 29
lasagna in a bun, 34
mini chimichangas, 11
pepperoni stromboli, 61
sloppy joe calzones, 87
sloppy joes for 8 dozen, 36
taco burgers, 32
tasty burritos, 68
zesty tacos, 82

HAM
breakfast biscuits 'n' eggs, 15
cordon bleu stromboli, 74
country ham sandwiches, 57
ham & apple grilled cheese sandwiches, 25
ham & cheese breakfast strudels, 19
ham 'n' cheese brunch strips, 14
ham and cheese calzones, 91
ham 'n' egg breakfast wraps, 21
ham and mango wraps, 76
ham and swiss bagels, 51
ham pinwheels, 8
ham salad croissants, 44
hawaiian ham salad pockets, 81
lunch-box "handwiches", 81
mini subs, 11
prosciutto egg panini, 18
sandwich for 12, 46
savory sandwich ring, 57
stuffed bread appetizers, 5
sweet 'n' sour pockets, 83
waffled monte cristos, 39

HOT SANDWICHES

aloha burgers, 28
barbecued chicken hoagies, 24
basil burgers, 23
bbq beef sandwiches, 35
bistro breakfast panini, 16
breaded turkey sandwiches, 29
breakfast biscuits 'n' eggs, 15
cajun burgers, 30
chicken pesto clubs, 30
chipotle bbq pork sandwiches, 38
coney dogs, 28
dad's quick bagel omelet sandwich, 14
egg salad english muffins, 13
freezer veggie burgers, 40
french dip sandwiches, 41
french toast supreme, 19
game day brats, 35
grilled bacon-tomato sandwiches, 31
grilled vegetable sandwich, 23
ham & apple grilled cheese sandwiches, 25
italian blts, 36
italian patty melts, 29
italian sausage sandwiches, 33
lasagna in a bun, 34
mustard turkey sandwiches, 33
open-faced cheesesteak sandwiches, 34
open-faced meatball sandwiches, 31
open-faced tuna melts, 37
open-faced turkey burgers, 25
pork tenderloin panini with fig port jam, 41
prosciutto egg panini, 18
provolone 'n' turkey sandwiches, 38
pulled pork sandwiches, 24
reuben grill, 26
sailor sandwiches with caesar mayo, 27
singapore satay sandwiches, 26
sloppy joes for 8 dozen, 36
stuffed pork burgers, 37
taco burgers, 32
tex-mex beef sandwiches, 40
waffled monte cristos, 39

MEATLESS SANDWICHES

avocado tomato wraps, 77
black bean 'n' corn quesadillas, 86
california wraps, 77
chickpea sandwich spread, 48
chocolate peanut butter sandwiches, 46
freezer veggie burgers, 40
fresh mozzarella sandwiches, 50
garbanzo bean pitas, 92
greek salad pitas, 99
grilled vegetable sandwich, 23
hearty veggie sandwiches, 59
mom's egg salad sandwiches, 55
nutty marmalade sandwiches, 44
pbj on a stick, 11
pear waldorf pitas, 84
portobello pockets, 85
spanish-style brunch wraps, 18
spinach 'n' broccoli enchiladas, 67
vegetarian hummus wraps, 74
walnut-cream cheese finger sandwiches, 6
zesty vegetarian tortillas, 76

MUSHROOMS

beefy swiss bundles, 95
freezer veggie burgers, 40
giant calzone, 92
mini beef wellingtons, 5
mini chicken salad croissants, 10
pepper steak quesadillas, 97
portobello pockets, 85
stuffed pork burgers, 37
zucchini pizza loaves, 90

NUTS & PEANUT BUTTER

asian chicken salad, 64
asian meatless wraps, 61
blts with raisin-avocado spread, 53
caramel cream crepes, 20
cashew turkey salad sandwiches, 54
cherry-chicken salad croissants, 56
chicken salad sandwiches, 49
chicken satay wraps, 66
chocolate-almond dessert crepes, 105
chocolate peanut butter sandwiches, 46
easy cherry strudels, 102
fruited turkey salad pitas, 83
fruity peanut butter pitas, 99
garbanzo bean pitas, 92
golden apple bundles, 101
gourmet deli turkey wraps, 69
ham salad croissants, 44
havarti turkey hero, 49
hazelnut apricot strudel, 107
mini chicken salad croissants, 10
nutty marmalade sandwiches, 44
pbj on a stick, 11
peanut butter ice cream sandwiches, 102
pear waldorf pitas, 84
singapore satay sandwiches, 26
turkey focaccia club, 43
waffled monte cristos, 39
walnut-cream cheese finger sandwiches, 6

OPEN-FACED SANDWICHES

crab salad tea sandwiches, 10
egg salad english muffins, 13
lemony shrimp sandwiches, 45
open-faced cheesesteak sandwiches, 34
open-faced meatball sandwiches, 31
open-faced tuna melts, 37
open-faced turkey burgers, 25

PEPPERS

chili chicken enchiladas, 64
fast fajita pita, 88
greek salad pitas, 99
grilled vegetable sandwich, 23
lime jalapeno turkey wraps, 65
pepper steak quesadillas, 97

PITAS & POCKETS

artichoke chicken pockets, 96
baked chicken chimichangas, 82
barbecued chicken quesadillas, 88
beef gyros, 81
beefy swiss bundles, 95
black bean 'n' corn quesadillas, 86

breakfast quesadillas, 20
cheeseburger pockets, 87
chili pockets, 89
crab salad pockets, 83
crescent sausage rolls, 21
easy cherry strudels, 102
fast fajita pita, 88
flatbread tacos with ranch sour cream, 84
french cheeseburger loaf, 96
fried chicken pitas, 98
fruited turkey salad pitas, 83
fruity peanut butter pitas, 99
garbanzo bean pitas, 92
giant calzone, 92
golden apple bundles, 101
greek chicken sandwiches, 89
greek salad pitas, 99
ham & cheese breakfast strudels, 19
ham and cheese calzones, 91
hawaiian ham salad pockets, 81
hearty sirloin pitas, 93
lunch-box "handwiches", 81
mango shrimp pitas, 91
mini beef wellingtons, 5
mini chimichangas, 11
mini greek burgers, 93
pear waldorf pitas, 84
pepper pork pockets, 95
pepper steak quesadillas, 97
portobello pockets, 85
puffy lobster turnovers, 6
reuben braids, 94
sausage & spinach calzones, 86
sausage sandwich squares, 98
seafood salad pitas, 89
sesame hot dogs, 86
sloppy joe calzones, 87
strawberry cheese bundles, 103
sweet 'n' sour pockets, 83
tender chicken pockets, 94
zesty tacos, 82
zucchini pizza loaves, 90

PORK

chipotle bbq pork sandwiches, 38
ham and cheese calzones, 91
pepper pork pockets, 95
pepperoni stromboli, 61
pork tenderloin panini with fig port jam, 41
pulled pork sandwiches, 24
shredded pork burritos, 79
stuffed pork burgers, 37

SALAMI, PASTRAMI & PEPPERONI

brickyard bistro sandwich, 56
mini muffuletta, 7
pastrami deli wraps, 76
reuben grill, 26
zucchini pizza loaves, 90

SAUSAGE & HOT DOGS

coney dogs, 28
crescent sausage rolls, 21
game day brats, 35
giant calzone, 92

alphabetical index

This index lists every recipe in alphabetical order, so you can easily find your favorite recipes.